THE POWER HOUSE

BY

CJ TANNER

Copyright © 2004 by CJ Tanner

The Power House
by CJ Tanner

Printed in the United States of America

ISBN 1-594678-61-8

All rights reserved solely by the author. The author guarantees all contents are original and do not infringe upon the legal rights of any other person or work. No part of this book may be reproduced in any form without the permission of the author. The views expressed in this book are not necessarily those of the publisher.

Unless otherwise indicted, Scripture is taken from the Holy Bible, New King James Version. Copyright © 1994 by Thomas Nelson Publishers.

The Best of Andrew Murray on Prayer
2000 by Barbour Publishing

Shout To The Lord
Words and Music by Darlene Zsheck- 1993

Turn Around
Words and Music by Harry Belafonte, Alan Greene, and Malvina Reynolds

Change My Heart O' God
Words and Music by Eddie Espinosa

This Could Be The Start of Something Big
Words and Music by Steve Allen

www.xulonpress.com

*In Memory of my mother:
Nina Griffith Thomas.*

ENDORSEMENTS OF THE POWER HOUSE

"After a lifetime of ministry there are not many surprises left—always new joys and new sorrows, but not many complete surprises. Imagine my surprise when I was so captivated by CJ Tanner's book that I read it through in one unbroken sitting. *The Power House* is a remarkable story of a pastor and wife who witnessed the life-transforming power of God. Each chapter is like a fresh visitation of the Holy Spirit. I commend this novel to you. It will interest, awaken, and challenge you. It is a life lived in constant awareness that God not only cares, but that He is intimately and powerfully involved in the lives of people."

<u>Dr. Dan Baumann (Pastor and Author)</u>
"Confronted By love: God's Principle for Daily Living"
    "Dare To Believe"
    "An Introduction To Contemporary Preaching"
    "Extraordinary Living For Ordinary People"
    "All Originality Makes a Dull Church"
    "Which Way To Happiness"
    "Clearing Life's Hurdles"

"I want writers to help me board a plane and fly toward a land I know about, but can see from the air of their words in new ways. That is how I felt reading *The Power House*. I hear the conversations and observe the facial expressions. In her narrative, CJ Tanner gives readers a glance at real issues about life's difficulties and ultimate victory. She helps us learn to endure and face what awaits us, knowing the ultimate victory. Get on the plane and enjoy the flight."

Chris Maxwell, Pastor and Author www.chrismaxwellweb.com
"Beggars Can Be Chosen"
"Another Day Along The Way"

"In her book, *The Power House*, CJ Tanner captures the real life of the average pastor in the sense that there are always problems and challenges involved with the people that God puts in the pastor's life. Her emphasis on prayer being essential to the Christian walk is clear. The best thing about this story is that you want to see what the characters are going to do next—on the next page, and in the next chapter. I encourage you to give strong consideration to reading this book!

Timothy B. Wildmon, President/ American Family Association
Author: (Humor) *"I Wonder What Noah Did With The Woodpeckers"*
"My Life As A Half-Baked Christian"

CHAPTER ONE

Joseph DuPriest was five years old when he first felt the hand of God upon him. Like some children, he had heard about God, but he was not taken to church. His parents had died in an automobile accident when he was four. After that, he lived with his grandparents. His grandmother would tell him, "Joseph, you wash your hands now. God doesn't like dirty hands at the table." She would say things to him like, "Joseph, you must be good. God doesn't like bad little boys."

If he was particularly good that day, she would tuck him in that night and say, "Joseph, you were very good today. God and His angels are smiling at you." But, she never took him to church, so his knowledge of God extended only to the references his grandmother made.

Joseph could still vividly remember the day he met God. He was lying beneath a huge pine tree in the meadow near where his grandparents lived. He had ventured farther than usual that day, and had stopped to rest before going back home.

He had asthma, and was beginning to feel an attack coming on. He was tired from running. The wind was blowing very hard, and breathing was becoming difficult. He could feel his heart beginning to race.

Joseph began to panic, his fear coming from having had attacks like this before. He did not have his medication with him, and he was frightened.

Due to his difficulty in breathing, he knew he could not make it back home, or even call out for help from his grandfather, who was supposed to have been watching him.

Joseph remembered stopping to sit beneath the tree, then lying back, hoping he would be able to breathe better. He remembered closing his eyes, tossing and turning, as he began to lose his ability to breathe.

Suddenly, he felt a slight pressure on his arm. It was as though someone had laid a hand on his shoulder. He thought he heard someone say, "Lie still, Joseph." He opened his eyes, but he did not see anyone.

He saw clouds moving above his head, and saw the tree being swayed by the wind. He lay very still. He felt calmer, and his pulse began to beat steadier.

In a few moments, he was able to stand and walk back through the meadow to his grandparents' house. He smiled as he looked up into the sky.

Even though he was only five years old, Joseph DuPriest knew he had felt the hand of God touch him, helping him in his time of need. From that day on, he felt very special, as though he was being watched over by an unseen being.

He did not tell anyone about the experience right away, but kept it to himself for quite some time. He would always count that day as the beginning of his personal relationship with the Almighty.

Laughter was the weapon Joseph chose early in life to enable him to deal with his childhood years. Things were not easy for him, having lost his parents at such a young age. His life was quite different from the other children's, not only because he didn't have his parents, but that he had to be careful what he did in order not to bring on an asthma attack.

His grandparents were not wealthy, and Joseph learned

early not to long for things he couldn't have, but to be content with what he had.

As it turned out, it was a good policy, one that he kept for his entire life. Even though he eventually outgrew the problem of childhood asthma, he kept to self-discipline and moderation in most avenues of his life. He understood about the frailty of life, and he carried this with him from his youth to his later years.

Having suffered illness as a child, Joseph learned to have compassion for others who were not healthy, or were afflicted in some other way.

There are people who clown all the time, sometimes at the expense of others. Joseph was not that way, even as a child. Even though he laughed a lot, his sensitivity to people showed, especially in his laughter.

If he saw someone in a situation that was making them uncomfortable or embarrassed, he went out of his way to change to a lighter note, usually finding a way to put a smile back on the faces of those involved. It was no wonder that Joseph was either liked, or loved, by those who knew him.

As he grew older, his love and his knowledge of the Lord strengthened. Joseph hardly ever missed a Sunday at church. He gave his life to the Lord, and when he was older, he committed himself to becoming a minister to bring others to know Christ.

After he was ordained, Joseph preached whenever and wherever he could. While preaching at one of the churches, he met Eva Simmons. They dated for almost one year, then, they married.

Eva, like Joseph, loved the Lord, and wanted to serve Him. Together, they began a ministry.

A local retailer offered them a community room to use for their services. At first, the room was adequate; however, the numbers coming to hear Joseph preach grew rapidly. Joseph was grateful for the space provided by the retailer, but realized they would soon need a larger space. He and Eva had begun to pray diligently for God's will in providing a larger building.

Their ministry was without affiliation with other churches. Therefore, the church received no financial support from any of the denominations.

Joseph felt led by God to start a church, preaching from the Bible alone, using life's lessons he had learned from it. He also used examples from the experiences of others that he knew of from his years of Christian counseling.

Joseph DuPriest was affectionately called Pastor Joe by his congregation.

The Lord had blessed Joseph and Eva with two sons. Paul was the oldest, and Joey came along a year later.

After Joey was born, Pastor Joe kidded with the congregation that he and Eva were growing the church and everyone needed to pray for the Lord to provide a larger space. The truth was that they hardly had room for those who came to hear him preach, and the church was continuing to grow.

This had been one of those rare Sundays when Joseph was struggling to get through his sermon. There were so many thoughts going through his head, he wasn't sure what avenue to take next. All at once, Joseph felt the hand of God upon him. He closed his eyes while making the altar call, and suddenly, the familiar touch was there. He stood, pleading the case for Christ, as he always did, at the end of his sermon. When he felt God's touch, he waited for the word he knew God was about to give him.

The Lord gave him the word - *forgiveness*. Upon hearing the word from the Lord, he announced that God was particularly calling that day for hearts to be mended, but that it would have to begin with forgiveness. He knew that God was dealing with someone at that moment. He asked for that person, or persons, to come forward so he could pray with them. When he opened his eyes, the altar was filled with

The Power House

people who were convicted by the Holy Spirit to come forward. They were seeking prayer to help them to forgive, and some to ask forgiveness for themselves. They wanted the new and clean heart that was being offered them by God through his messenger, Joseph DuPriest.

"Thank you, Lord, for these people who have given their lives to you today," said Joseph, as he sat alone in his makeshift study, half an hour after the altar call. "Thank you that you come to me when I need you. Thank you that, even when I am at a loss for the right words, Father, you never are. I am so thankful that you taught me at an early age to listen for your voice."

He looked up as he heard Eva knocking on the study door.

"Hold on a second. I'm coming, Eva," he said, as he rose from his desk to go to the door. "Let's get those boys and go have some lunch," he said, smiling at his wife, as he took her arm.

"We have five new members as of this morning, sweetheart. Five new souls committed to serving Christ," he announced to his wife, with a big smile.

"I am so happy to have five new members, Joe. Remind me, though, to order some more chairs. Have you noticed that we are running out of chairs, as well as a place to put them?"

"It's a good problem to have, Eva, dear. But, we must continue to pray that God will provide a larger building. He keeps sending us souls to save. They will need chairs to sit in or the souls will be *standing* on their soles," he chuckled.

Eva laughed along with him, at his little pun.

The next day at the church began with a paper cut. Making her way down the hall to get a bandage from the first aid kit, Anna, Pastor Joe's secretary, noticed a light under the door to his study. The study was usually locked, but now it stood slightly open. It was much too early for the pastor to be there. Tentatively, Anna eased open the door,

The Power House

believing she was the only person in the building.

The strangest sight lay before her eyes. In the pastor's chair were his pants, upright, as though the Pastor were sitting there. The shirt was folded so that the elbow was draped on the corner of the desk, just as the pastor always sat when working on his Sunday sermon.

After a jolt to her system, Anna realized this display was acting out of the joke Pastor Joe always made. He would tease that he worked so much at his desk, one day the Rapture would occur as he was working, and someone would look for him and find only his clothing.

At the moment she started to smile broadly, she heard laughter coming from behind the door. Pulling the door open wider, Anna saw Pastor Joe with his hand over his mouth, trying not to laugh out loud. He had to dodge, as Anna could not resist swatting at him with the papers in her hand, as she laughed along with him at his early morning joke.

The day that had begun on an unexpected note with a paper cut was continued with the usual laughter and sense of humor of the well-loved pastor.

This day was to be one of the times when Joseph realized he would need to use the sensitivity and compassion given him by God. He was meeting with Paula Chance, a young wife and mother whose life had taken a sharp turn, as he was told, not for the better.

Her two year old son, Sam, had died, suddenly, from complications of a high fever. Joseph did not know Paula or her son, however, he had been asked to meet with her by a friend of hers who was a member of his church.

Joseph returned to his study that afternoon, closed the door, and went to a chair in his favorite place by the window to pray for the meeting that would occur within the hour.

"Dear Heavenly Father," Joseph prayed. "Please clear my mind, and my heart of all things concerning myself. Father, leave only space for me to concentrate on the sorrow of my sister in Christ Jesus, who is coming to me for counsel. Please give me the words that you would have her hear, as if she were coming to you, kneeling at your feet, and pouring out her problems to you. Let my eyes see, my ears hear, and my lips speak only wisdom divined from you, my Heavenly Father. I pray this, in the name of Jesus. Amen."

As Joseph rose from his knees in his place of prayer by the window, he glanced out to see a young woman getting out of an automobile. He noticed, as she walked towards the entry, that her face was sad, and she was very thin. She was walking slowly up the walk, with her hands clasped together in front of her.

Pastor Joe took a deep breath, put his faith in God, and went to greet her.

He stepped to the entry in time to open the door for the young woman, as she entered the building.

He extended his hand to her.

"Good morning. I am Pastor Joseph DuPriest. Everyone calls me Pastor Joe."

She reached out and took the hand he offered. He noticed how frail her hand felt in his own.

"I am Paula Chance. Thank you for agreeing to see me today."

"I understand that one of our members suggested you meet with me," said Pastor Joe. "Won't you join me in my study, so we can talk privately?"

Paula Chance looked into his kind face, and slightly shook her head.

He opened the door for her and indicated that she sit on the sofa. He took a seat opposite her in a chair. For a brief moment, there was no exchange of words, only the sound of their breathing was heard in the room. Then, Pastor Joe reached and took her hand.

"It goes without saying that I am sorry for the loss of your young son," he began. "But, I know in my heart that you did not come here today for sympathy. I believe you came for answers."

Looking up at Pastor Joe, Paula slowly nodded her head to indicate that he was correct about what he had said. She spoke only one word, softly, with a frown forming on her face.

"Why?"

This was the one question that Pastor Joe had anticipated. Having served as a pastor for many years, he had heard that question over and over from loved ones when someone died unexpectedly. He had pondered the same thing, after losing his parents when he was a young child. He knew there was only one way to answer her question. It was the only truth about a sudden death that he, or anyone else, for that matter, could honestly give.

"We do not know why, Mrs. Chance. Nobody but God truly knows why. If I told you anything other than that, I would be inventing reasons that could not hold water."

Mrs. Chance looked at him, quizzically. The answer he had just given her was not at all what she had anticipated.

"The Bible tells us in Ecclesiastes that, *"To everything there is a season and a time for every purpose under heaven*: - *a time to be born and a time to die."* I believe that every person has an appointed time to die, the time known only to God Himself. And, the reason they are to die at their appointed time is His reason alone, as well. In time, all will be revealed to us that know Him. Are you a believer, Mrs. Chance?"

"Oh, yes, Pastor Joe. I believe in the Lord, with all my heart. It's funny, but I haven't felt the anger at Him some people say they have when they have lost someone. I just have all these unanswered questions. Why did he take Sam? He was only two years old. He never had a chance to live. He was doing fine, until the morning he got that awful fever. They couldn't get the fever to break. Then, he lost consciousness and never recovered."

Tears began to flow down Paula's cheeks.

Pastor Joe patted her hand and said, "I wish I had answers that could soothe you. I wish I could just tell you what some ministers say. That the child was such an angel, that God couldn't live in Heaven without him any longer, and called him back to be with Him there. Mrs. Chance, I can't tell you that, because I don't know that to be true. That's what you are looking for here this morning, isn't it? The truth about why Sam died."

"Yes, that is what I need to know, in my heart."

Pastor Joe looked into her eyes and said, "Maybe we don't know why, but God had a reason for allowing it to happen. There is a reason. One that, because you love the Lord, you will one day know. By faith alone, you need to believe that one fact. God loves Sam, and He loves you. He knows your grief, and He wants you to come to Him for comfort. You have been grieving for quite some time, I understand."

"A year and a half," she answered softly. "I have gone to other ministers, to counselors, and it's a funny thing, you know. Some of them told me just what you said you *wouldn't* tell me. About Sam being such a little angel, that God wanted him back with Him."

"Do you know, Pastor Joe, that statement has kept me up walking the floor many nights, wondering if the God I love would be so cruel to give me my baby for two years to love and cherish, only to know He planned all along to take him back. If that was true, then that would mean He put me through this anguish intentionally," Paula said.

She covered her face with her hands, as she finished talking.

Pastor Joe kept silent, knowing she was on her way to recovery. She had begun to talk about losing Sam. She was not willing to accept all the things she had been told to accept, as to the reason she lost her child, the things that didn't make any sense to her.

He knew that the healing process had to begin with her being able to talk about Sam's dying, openly, seeking answers to her confusion and her pain.

"Why, one counselor even told me that something was going to happen to Sam in the future that would have been so devastating, that God went ahead and took him early, to save everyone the additional grief," Paula said.

She looked at Pastor Joe, and shrugged her shoulders.

"Whatever that means," she said. "But, that bothered me too. Not only did I have to think about losing Sam, but being in the emotional state I have been in, I started lying awake at night, imaging what terrible things might have happened to him, if he had lived."

Paula sat looking at Pastor Joe, shaking her head slowly.

"Pastor Joe, that is so hard to swallow. Those reasons they kept giving me. You know what else? I had come to the conclusion that it was because of something I did wrong, that, I didn't deserve to have that sweet child. That, maybe God was punishing me for something I should have done, or something I actually did."

She began to sob, overcome by all the thoughts she had swirling in her head, about the loss of her child.

Pastor Joe shook his head and lifting her face with his fingers, wiped away her tears.

"Mrs. Chance," he said. "Can you accept that we just won't truly know the answer of *why* while we are still here on earth? That God doesn't have children die to inflict punishment on the parents? That's not my God. That's not the loving, caring Father God I know. Do *you* truly picture God that way?"

"No, I don't," said Paula, softly, slowly shaking her head. "I know our God to be a loving God. I know there *will* come a judgment. And, in my heart of hearts, I found it difficult to believe He would punish me for *my* sins by taking Sam."

"Can you accept what I am telling you now as the truth, Mrs. Chance?"

"Pastor Joe, please, just call me Paula."

"Then, Paula, can you accept, in faith, that there was a reason? Can you also accept that you won't know that reason until the day God Himself reveals it to you? If you can do that, you can get past this and go on with your life, remembering Sam as the sweet little boy he was. Recognizing that, it does hurt beyond anyone's understanding other than your own, and begin to deal with it on that level?"

"It's the only answer I have been given that makes any sense. I can honestly tell you right now that I feel better, hearing you say the loving things about God today. Hearing you tell me that maybe there aren't going to be any answers about *why* right away. That may seem strange to you, but it does seem easier to handle than all the suppositions I have been put through by some of your learned colleagues."

"Then, if you accept that one fact, Paula, please understand when I tell you this one, as well. I told you before, that in Ecclesiastes it says, *"There is a time and a purpose for everything under heaven."* That goes for grieving, too. You have grieved for Sam for a year and a half. The fact is, you are still here. Your husband is still here. Your other two children are still here. You need to acknowledge them, and to start a new life, a different life than when Sam was here, but a new life that includes them. And, especially one that includes yourself."

Paula wiped away the tears on her face and blew her nose with the tissues that Pastor Joe handed her.

She looked at him and said, "You know, that is the one thing I think I have felt guilty about. That I get to see the sun come up every day, smell the new grass mowed in the park, feel the wind on my face, the things that Sam loved."

"That's very normal to feel that way, Paula. But, there is also a reason God left you here. There are things He wants you to do. You have a life to live. There are people who need you. *Yes*, you need to remember Sam. Cry when you need to. But, Paula, remember those who are still here, and, that includes you, as well."

"I realize that I have neglected my family in my own grief, Pastor Joe. I hide away in my room. I make someone else answer the door when my well-meaning friends come by to see me. As I sit here right now, I feel a peace from God that has begun to well up in my soul. But, along with that peace about Sam, I have to admit that I have been remiss in my duties to my family."

Paula kept her head down and her eyes closed as she spoke these words.

"Well, Paula, you have now acknowledged that you have left them out. From this moment on, put that time in your life behind you. If you tell them how you have been feeling, and that you are sorry you have left them out of your grieving, you will see that they understand. In fact, your daughter is the one who asked your friend to see if you would come visit with me. She has been very concerned, even though she is so young."

Paula looked up, surprised at what Pastor Joe was saying about her daughter having asked for help for her. Noting her surprise, he continued.

"So as you step out the front door, *see* the sun, *smell* the new grass that was mowed fresh this morning, and *feel* the breeze that is blowing out there. Think about your family and what you can do for them today. The most important thing in their lives right now is to have you back. The wife, the mother, and the friend they are all missing. Can you do that, Paula?"

Paula took a deep breath and held her head up high, looking at the ceiling.

The Power House

"You know, I would have thought it impossible when I came up that walk this morning, but yes, I think I can do that."

"As I said, it is strange, but I feel the peace of God around me at this very moment. I know He can get me through this. And, you are right. I have to go on living. I have been living, but it was as though everything has been about my grief. I have examined every reason I could think of and every reason someone gave me as to why Sam had to die."

"As I sit here, I really feel ashamed of the fact that, though my family has been so supportive, I have not shown them much in the past eighteen months except my own tears. They hurt, too. I pray that God will let me say and do the right things from this very moment to put things back together, so we can go forward."

The words Paula spoke at the end of the conversation were those Pastor Joe had been waiting to hear. He knew, without a doubt, that God had given him the right words to say to Paula. He knew she was reacting to what God gave him to say to this grieving mother. The words were of a loving Father, comforting his child in her hour of need.

Pastor Joe waited until Paula had finished talking and then said, "Paula, please let me pray with you now."

Paula reached and took both of Pastor Joe's hands in her own and said, "I am ready, Pastor Joe."

"Our dear and gracious heavenly Father," Pastor Joe began. "Thank you for your holy presence with us here in this room today. Thank you, Lord, that Paula believes in you and acknowledges that there are just simply things in life that happen, for which we cannot possibly know the reasons. But, that you do, Father. And, you are in control of our lives, if we will only allow you to be. I pray now that Paula will continue to feel your Holy Spirit bringing peace into her life. For, Lord, *you* are the Great Comforter."

"I pray that she will walk in your presence, not only this day, but for the rest of her days. That her family will sense the peace you have given her, and that their lives will be enriched as a family from this day forward. In the name of Jesus, we ask these things. Amen."

Pastor Joe accompanied Paula to her car. He asked her to keep in touch with him, and invited her to bring her family to church on Sunday morning. Paula assured him that was something she would really like to do.

As she drove away, Pastor Joe walked over to a park bench that had been placed underneath a large oak tree. The bench was beautifully carved, with an inscription reading, *"With God, All Things Are Possible."* The bench had been donated by a church member who had received an answer from the Lord to a problem that was seemingly insurmountable. Pastor Joe noticed how the seat on the bench was worn from people stopping by to sit on the bench and pray.

He thought about Paula Chance. He again prayed that she would come to realize what the inscription on the bench meant to her in her present situation.

He thought of the responsibility he had in shepherding his flock. He thought of their need for a larger building.

So many in his congregation had problems in their lives, and he constantly prayed for the Lord to give him the wisdom and strength to counsel and lead them.

He thought of his own life, his wife and children. He began to thank God for all he had been given.

CHAPTER TWO

Two months later, the Lord answered Pastor Joe and Eva's prayers for a larger building. The superintendent of the local high school came to several of the services. He saw how crowded the community room was, with all the people who had come to hear Pastor Joe preach.

He had an idea, and that week, took it to the school board. His idea was to offer the old high school auditorium to be used for church services, at no charge to the church.

The building had been abandoned for several years, and was of no use to the school. The church would have to refurbish part of it, but it would be put to a good use. The board agreed to let Pastor Joe and his congregation use the building, under those terms. The church was extremely grateful for the use of the facility. They certainly needed the space.

Pastor Joe had prayed about a name for the church. He felt strongly in his spirit that, for some reason, the Lord told him that, for now, he was to put *no name* to the church.

The building was dedicated as a church the first Sunday after the refurbishing was completed. The attendance was excellent that day, and for the first time in quite some time, there were enough seats for everyone.

"You may all be seated," said Pastor Joe, to the congregation, as they applauded his morning greeting. "And *that* is really something we can thank God for, isn't it?"

He smiled, and could hear some in the congregation laughing, as everyone caught his joke about the ample amount of seats that morning.

Then, Pastor Joe became serious about what he was about to present. His demeanor changed to quiet and reverent. The congregation followed suit.

"The service is going to be slightly different this morning. I want to invite those dedicated to the Lord to share their experiences of what God has done in your life. We have had testimonies on Sunday evenings, rather than Sunday mornings. However, the Lord has called me to ask people to give testimonies this morning based on specific subjects."

"As I read the scripture and call out the topic, I want to ask that you search your heart for the testimony from your life that relates to this topic."

"If the Lord leads you to share this testimony with the congregation, it will be because someone needs to hear what you have experienced. Their life may well be impacted by what you have to share."

"People, I beseech you. Please be sensitive to what the Holy Spirit is telling you, and if He inspires you to come forward, then be obedient to His calling."

At that moment, Pastor Joe stepped to a side podium that had been set up to the right of the regular one in the center of the platform at the altar. He left the regular one free for the speakers he knew the Lord would provide that morning.

"Before I read the first scripture, I must tell you that there is a reason for this topic being first. The Lord specifically gave me these topics, and I felt, in my spirit, that this is one of the most important ones."

"The Lord will have someone today testify about a close experience you have had with Him. Your testimony will touch the hearts of others that need to hear it."

"People, please listen to what the Lord is saying, as we begin with the testimonies. The Lord will show the testimony that is meant for you to give, or the one that is meant for you to hear. Praise be to God."

"The first topic is *humility*. The scripture the Lord gave me to read for the testimony is from Matthew 18:3-5:

"Assuredly, I say to you, unless you are converted and become as little children, you will by no means enter the kingdom of heaven. Therefore, whoever humbles himself as this little child is the greatest in the kingdom of heaven. Whoever receives one little child like this in My name receives Me."

At that point, Pastor Joe stopped reading. He sat the Bible down on top of the podium and put his hands together in prayer- like fashion, and held them to his lips, head bowed.

No one in the church said a word. It was very quiet, all heads bowed in prayer.

The stillness lasted for a full minute. Everyone sat with their heads bowed, and their eyes closed, searching their hearts about the scripture Pastor Joe had just read. Suddenly, a soft voice could be heard speaking into the microphone at the podium in the center of the platform at the altar.

"This scripture has to be for me. There are many ways to humble yourself, but the specific scripture given to Pastor Joe by the Lord tells me it can only be what God Himself revealed to me ten years ago."

Members of the congregation looked up to see the young woman who was speaking. It was Nancy West, one of the youth leaders.

"As most of you who know me already know, I work in special education at the local grade school. About ten years ago, I was a pharmaceutical representative. I did not walk with the Lord like I try to now. Most of my time on Sundays was spent lounging around the house in my pajamas, reading the Sunday paper and going to football parties in the afternoons."

"I always heard people talking about how the Lord had changed their lives, how the Lord spoke to them. But, until then, it had never happened to me. Sure, I acknowledged God, but I didn't want to spend my free time going to church to worship him. I traveled so much that it always turned out that Sunday was my only day off. Well, one day something happened that turned my life around, made me examine myself. And I can tell you right now, I didn't like what I saw."

Nancy paused and looked down at her shoes. Then she looked directly at the congregation.

"One day," she continued, "I was asked to go on a sales call to a local nursing home. I normally did not have to do that, because I had a sales territory that only included physicians' offices. This doctor that needed to talk to me about one of our products was going to be at the nursing home all that day. So, he asked if I would meet him there. I was aggravated that I had to change my whole schedule that day, but I said "okay", I would meet with him that afternoon."

"This happened to be one of those days that wasn't a bad hair day. I had on my favorite suit. I was about fifteen pounds slimmer than I am now."

Everyone in the audience laughed at that remark, along with Nancy herself.

"Well, anyway, I was feeling pretty good about myself, and I went tripping along in my little high heel shoes, feeling more than a little put out with this doctor for having me come all the way out to a nursing home to see him."

"When I got there, as luck would have it, *or so I thought*, he was in with a patient who was having some complications, so I had to wait. I am here to tell you today, it wasn't *as luck would have it*. It turned out to be *as God would have it*."

At this point, Nancy had the attention of everyone in the

The Power House

congregation. Pastor Joe walked backwards to a chair behind the podium where he was standing. He could tell there was quite a bit more to the story. He took a seat, continuing to gaze at Nancy West. He was as interested as everyone else.

"There was no place to sit, and the nurse asked me to stand outside in the hallway," continued Nancy. "Across the hall from where I was waiting for this doctor, was a room full of little tiny babies, tied in their wheelchairs with diapers. They were little *water head* babies, they used to call them. It was really scary to me to see all those tiny children tied in their chairs with diapers. Some of them were drooling down their chins, and just staring straight ahead."

"One of the babies was sitting closer to the door than the others, and he started making this noise - "Aye, aye, aye."

Nancy paused, thinking about the child she was telling about. Tears began to well up in her eyes, as she thought of the child. Then, she cleared her throat and started speaking, in a more strained voice.

"At that moment, I wanted to be anywhere but where I was. This child kept looking right at me and saying the same thing - "aye, aye, aye."

"I would look up at the ceiling, and then I would check my appointment book. I would look at my watch, anything to keep from looking into that room. And, especially to keep from looking at that one baby that kept staring at me, and making that noise."

Nancy shook her head and looked down at her feet, again. As she looked back up, her expression changed, and her voice became softer.

"All of a sudden, I felt the hand of God on me. No, I mean, I *really* felt the hand of God on my body. It was as though someone touched me from behind. As though He laid a hand on my shoulder, and pushed me to my knees right in front of that baby. Me, in my three hundred dollar suit, with my cute little hairdo, and my professional attitude. I found myself kneeling there, looking eye to eye with that baby, and I took his head that was much bigger than his body, in my hands. I smiled at him and I said, "Hi."

"You know what he did?" she asked, with a sob in her voice.

She choked up as she was telling this part of the story. She struggled to begin again.

"He said, "AYE", and he broke out into the biggest smile I have ever seen. You see, that was all he wanted. He wanted me to acknowledge his presence. He was trying all the time to say, "Hi."

"I cried right there in the hallway when I realized how shallow I had been in my thinking about this child. How terrible my attitude had been about all those children. I felt so ashamed."

"The nurse came out the door, where the doctor was with his patient, and told me he would have to see me another day. I said, "That's fine; tell him I'll call him." She went back in with the doctor, and I knelt in front of the baby. I kissed him on the top of his head. Again, another one of those big beautiful smiles, and - "aye, aye, aye."

"I said, "Forgive me, you sweet little angel, and may God bless you."

"He just gave me another sweet smile."

"I practically ran out of that building that day," she said, wiping her eyes with the back of her hand.

"When I got outside, I was so weak, I could barely stand. I dropped my briefcase beside the car."

"I looked up into a bright beautiful sky, and I said, "Thank you, God! Thank you for this beautiful day. Thank you that I am healthy enough to enjoy it. Thank you for opening my eyes to someone that has many more problems than I do, but can still smile that beautiful smile for everyone."

"You see, I was so full of myself when I went into that

The Power House

building. I was admiring my reflection in the glass of the door when I went in, thinking how good I looked that particular day. I could use a little humility, couldn't I?"

She laughed a little.

Then, very soberly, she said, "God chose a tiny, malformed little baby to humble me."

She paused to gather her composure. Everyone was very quiet in the auditorium.

"I felt sick to my stomach when I left there, thinking how ugly my thoughts had been about having to change my schedule. How I had wanted my friends to see my cute new suit, and about how angry I had been that I had to change my lunch plans."

"I was sick to my stomach because of my own trivial, selfish thoughts. That I was so shallow, I didn't want to even look at those babies in there."

"But, when I came out, I wasn't the same person. I have not been the same person, since God opened my eyes that day. He made me see myself for what I was, and I didn't like what I saw."

I got in my car, and I bowed my head, and asked the Lord to forgive me.

You see, that day he taught me a valuable lesson. He taught me humility. And, he did it through a sweet little child."

"So, you see, even if you are a tiny baby, with a bigger head than most, one smile can totally *change* someone's life. God can use anyone to do His will."

"I am here to tell you, people, that day changed my entire life. Because of what happened to me, I quit my job and began working with special education children. I don't make the money I used to make in pharmaceutical sales, but the reward is much greater. I can stand here and honestly tell you that I thank Him for that day."

Nancy turned to Pastor Joe.

"Thank you, Pastor Joe, for bringing that day back to my mind. I need to be reminded more often about how good it is to be humble. I know we all do, and that there is someone here today that God wanted to hear that story. I pray He will use my testimony to His glory. Would you mind reading that scripture again?"

Pastor Joe came back to where his Bible lay on the podium. He looked down at the Bible and read, once again:

"Assuredly, I say to you, unless you are converted and become as little children, you will by no means enter the kingdom of heaven. Therefore, whoever humbles himself as this little child is the greatest in the kingdom of heaven. Whoever receives one little child like this in My name receives Me."

The silence continued as Nancy West took her seat. She noticed some wiping tears from their eyes, and others avoiding looking at her, their heads still bowed.

Pastor Joe said, "Thank you, Nancy, for being sensitive to the Holy Spirit, and being obedient to Him in sharing your story with us. There is someone here, maybe more than one, whose heart or hearts you touched today. My prayer is that we will *all* come to understand the spirit of humility, as a little child, that the Lord calls us to, in order to enter the kingdom of heaven."

"I will not ask you to raise your hand if you felt that story was meant for you. I will ask you, though, to reflect on what you heard and search your heart for how it can change your life."

Pastor Joe paused for a moment. Then, he turned a page in his Bible and began speaking.

"The next topic for testimony today is *self-control*. There are many scriptures in the Bible about self-control, but for some reason the Lord told me the testimony that will be heard today is about this scripture I am about to read. The scripture the Lord gave me for this testimony is from Proverbs 10: 1:

"A wise son makes a glad father, but a foolish son is the grief of his mother."

Once again, Pastor Joe placed the Bible on the podium and took a seat, hands folded in prayer. Again, there was silence; however, this silence lasted longer than the last one. Pastor Joe sat there, knowing there was a testimony that was to be given, waiting for the Lord to stir the heart of the one to give it.

A shuffling noise broke the silence as the microphone was adjusted to fit the height of a tall, young black man who had come to the podium. His name was Jacob Carter, and he had been coming to the church for about six months.

His voice was trembling, as he addressed the congregation.

"I don't want to do this," he said, looking around, as he finished adjusting the microphone.

"In fact, I got out of my seat to leave, because I felt something so heavy on me when Pastor Joe read that scripture that I thought my chest would burst. When I got up to leave, the Lord turned me away from the door, and back in the direction of the platform I am standing on. I know that I have to share this story with all of you this morning. It seems the Lord has a hold on me right now. I couldn't leave here if I wanted to."

No one in the congregation moved, or said anything, as the young man crouched to a squatted position and rocked back and forth on his heels a couple of times, covering his eyes with one hand. There obviously was something heavy on his heart, and this was going to be difficult for him to do. Then, regaining his composure, he stood and addressed the congregation, speaking into the microphone.

"If I had been that wise son, I would not have brought the grief to my mother that I did. But, I wasn't wise. I was anything *but* wise."

"People, you aren't looking at one of those statistics you

hear about. You know what I mean, the statistics where young black men are only raised by their mothers. I'm not one of those statistics. You see, I had a father."

As he said the last word, "father", his voice broke. Jacob stopped and put his hands over his face, weeping noisily. Then, he wiped his nose, and began speaking again.

"In fact, I had a wonderful father. The problem was, I did not recognize that until it was too late. My father was a bookkeeper. I always thought he was one of those "nerds" because he kept that pocket pencil thing in his shirt pocket all the time. He worked every day except Saturday and Sunday, and when I was little, he and my mother would take me to ballgames and movies. We went to church on Sunday's."

"Man, I used to love Sunday school. We got to make neat things."

He laughed, nervously.

"And, I loved the songs we learned there. Those were some great songs."

"But, like a lot of the young men now days, I went the wrong way when I turned thirteen. I started running with the wrong crowds, doing things I shouldn't do. My mother was worried all the time, and we always got into a fight when I would finally come home. I don't just mean I was late for dinner. I didn't come home until three or four in the morning."

He stopped and took a deep breath, noticing the reaction of some of those in the congregation. Then he continued.

"Naturally, I didn't do too well in school, so that didn't help things with my parents, either. I would sneak out during the night."

"I see some of you people looking around at each other. Let me tell you something. If you want to do something bad enough, when you are a kid, you will find a way to do it. Don't blame my parents. It wasn't their fault. It was mine. I was way out of control."

He stepped back and cracked his knuckles, looking at

The Power House

the floor. He waited a moment, then, he stepped back to the microphone.

"One night, I was sixteen years old, and I thought I was a *man*. Nobody was going to tell *me* what to do."

He stopped and shook his head.

"I sneaked into my parents' bedroom while my mother was cooking dinner, and started getting some money out of her purse to go out and buy some dope. Yeah, I was into that, too. Anyway, she came in the bedroom about that time, and she caught me stealing from her. She told me to put the money back, but I wouldn't do it. She kind of wrestled with me, and I shoved her into the wall. She hit her head, and started crying, but I didn't care. I just had to have that fix, and to get it, I had to have that money."

"Well, my father came home about then, and came in and saw my mother sitting against the wall, crying. He started towards me, and I just ran past him, and out the door. It was pouring rain, and I ran out into the rain to go buy my dope."

"I didn't know it at the time, but my mother had cut her head really bad when I shoved her, and my father was madder at me than he had ever been in his life. He took her to the emergency room, then, he took her home and put her to bed. Then, he got in the car and went to find me."

Jacob squeezed his eyes together with his hand, and started shaking his head.

"Well, like I said, it was raining that night. He went to the usual places I hung out. But, I figured that was where he would go, so I got my dope and sneaked up in the tree house he had made me when I was a little kid. It was a big one, a real nice one, and he had made it big enough for my friends to play up there with me. I knew he would never to think to look for me there. I was right about that, he didn't."

"The next thing I knew, there were police cars in our front yard, two of them, with their lights going. I couldn't believe my folks would call the police on me, even after what I had done. I figured all they would do is talk to me when I came home, about getting my act together, like they always did."

"All of a sudden, I heard my mother screaming. I got down out of the tree house and started running toward the house. I hadn't done the dope yet, thank God. The police were there to tell my mother that my father had hit a slick spot in the highway out there driving around in the dark in the rain, looking for me. He hit a telephone pole. He was killed instantly, they said."

Jacob really started crying at this point. Tears were flowing, and he tried to choke them back in order to continue speaking.

"You see, people, the last thing you could call me at the time was a *wise son*, and I *certainly* brought grief to my mother. All this happened because I had no self-control."

"That was four years ago. I am twenty years old now. Because of my foolishness, I lost a wonderful father that night, and my mother lost the husband she loved dearly."

"But, that night, I became a man, a different man. I threw away that dope. I threw away my so -called friends, and I changed my life."

"It was too late for him to see it, but I became the man my father wanted me to become. And most of all, I gave my heart to the Lord that my daddy used to take me to Sunday school to learn about. I told the Lord that I was His, if he would take me. I told Him to use me to help other kids not do what I did, when I was young and unwise. I have been trying to help troubled kids like I was, ever since that time."

All at once, down the aisle came an elegant, gray haired woman, walking slowly towards the front of the church. She had her arms open wide, and as she approached the platform, Jacob stepped forward to greet her with open arms.

It was his mother. She attended her own church, but Jacob had been asking her for months to visit his church with him. She had gone to her own church that day, but felt the urge to leave early, and come to her son's church. She had slipped into the back pew, during the last of Nancy's testimony. She knew now why she had chosen this particular day to visit her son's church.

She stepped up to the microphone, and said, "This is my son. He is right; he is now the man his father wanted him to be. I forgave him, the Lord forgave him, and I hope you can forgive him, too."

"This story is hard to hear, because it is where a lot of kids are these days. But, if Jacob's story can touch you, and change you before it is too late, then I thank God he had the courage to tell it to you today."

Jacob hugged his mother, then took her arm and started down the platform, but Pastor Joe asked them to wait.

He said, "After the last testimony, I told the congregation that you didn't have to raise your hand, if you felt this testimony was for you. I feel that the Holy Spirit is speaking to many of you out there this morning, after hearing what this young man had to say."

"If you hear the Lord speaking to you, and you want to change your life for the better, to turn your life around, because you are headed down a dead end street of self destruction, then I ask you to come forward right now, and let us pray for you. Get started this morning on the right path."

Pastor Joe stood beside Jacob and his mother, and waited. It only took a few moments before there were fourteen young men and women there, at the altar. They ranged in ages between thirteen and eighteen. Every single one of them was crying.

It seemed as though Jacob's testimony had touched many hearts. Pastor Joe was surprised to see who some of the young people were. But, he couldn't know what was going on in all their homes, or in their private lives. He did know that some of them sat sullenly in the pew on Sunday, and were nudged by their parents to stay awake.

As the young ones came down the aisle, their parents faces revealed their relief and joy at the step their children were taking this morning.

"I want to ask the elders of the church to come and meet these young people as they come forward, and pray with them, and that those in your seats pray along with us."

Elders stepped forward and went to each of the young men and women at the altar. They began to talk with each one, and to pray for their individual needs. The prayers continued for about ten minutes, then, Pastor Joe said, "I feel the Holy Spirit moving among us this morning. I feel there are other testimonies that need to be told, but I would like to wait until the evening services to share those. How many of you will commit to coming back this evening? Don't raise your hand, unless you really mean it."

The majority of the congregation raised their hands.

"Then, come back tonight and expect the Holy Spirit to welcome you when you enter these doors. May His peace be upon you the rest of this day. You are dismissed."

"I would like to ask these young people and their parents to stay for a brief meeting, if you don't mind. Will the parents please come forward, and stand beside your children?"

As the parents were coming to the front of the church to stand beside their children, Pastor Joe went to Jacob Carter.

"Jacob, when you gave your testimony, you said that you had given yourself to a service for the Lord to help save kids who were headed in the same direction you had been. Do you still mean that?"

Jacob shook his head and said, "Yes, sir, I mean that. I have been witnessing to anybody who was willing to listen to what I had to say. But, other than that, I haven't been able to do much."

"Jacob, we have a need for you right here in this church. I have been praying about how we could help the troubled youth of our city. Of course, we have a youth program here at our church, but it is not designed to counsel specifically with kids that are going in the wrong direction. I believe you are the man to help get this started. Are you willing to do that, or would you at least consider what I am asking you?"

"I don't need time to consider it, Pastor Joe. I want to do it, if you feel I am the person for it. I will do my best to help guide young people in the right direction."

"Then let's start with this group. How many of you are willing to make a commitment to come to the church and meet with Jacob at least once a week? There will be programs for you to learn about the dangers of drug use. There will be places for you to go, rather than the streets. And, there will be a caring person that understands where you are, and where you have been. But, the best thing is that he understands where you need to be," said Pastor Joe.

All of the young people who had stepped forward that morning raised their hands in response to Pastor Joe's question. They were all willing to accept the help that was being offered.

"And, will you parents commit to coming to counseling sessions here in the church at least once a week, along with your children? We have a Christian counselor who is one of our members, and he has already told me he would be willing to help put a program together. Will you be as bold as your children, and promise to do this to help them become wiser sons and daughters?"

All the parents raised their hands.

"Then, let us set a date right now and get this program started. Jacob, the ball is in your court. It's up to you to organize a meeting, and let's make sure it happens this week."

Within a few months, the new program became one of the strongest programs within the city. Many young people's lives were changed as a result of that single testimony from Jacob Carter. Once again, the Lord had used a situation to turn evil to good.

CHAPTER THREE

Pastor Joe sat in the study of the church, laughing so hard his sides were aching. Anna could hear him from down the hallway. She was used to him laughing, but rarely did she hear him all the way down the hallway from her office.

He had just begun talking with his latest two members, Janet and Jonathan Still. Jonathan ran the local funeral home. Janet was the director of nurses at the local hospital. They had been coming to the church for over a year, and had just acknowledged to Pastor Joe that they wanted to join.

As required by all new members, Pastor Joe asked to have a meeting with them before they were presented to the congregation, as new members. He wanted to make certain they understood the commitment they were about to make. Also, he wanted to see if there were any questions they might have about being members of the church.

Janet had been relating a story about when she and Jonathan were first married.

At that time, Jonathan was in training to become a funeral director, and she was in college studying for her master's degree in nursing.

They lived in a small apartment above the funeral home. One evening, Janet was telling Pastor Joe, they had a big argument. At the moment, neither was able to even remember what they were arguing about, but Janet did remember that ten minutes into the argument, Jonathan grew tired of arguing and went into the bathroom and shut the door.

After a few minutes of being in the bathroom, and listening to Janet yelling at him outside the door, Jonathan noticed that everything had suddenly gotten very quiet.

He ventured out the door and called for Janet. Not hearing a reply, he went into the kitchen. No Janet. He went into the living room, again, no Janet. He went downstairs, and there, lying on the red velvet sofa in the chapel, was his wife, all curled up with a blanket and a pillow.

The thing that was making Pastor Joe laugh so hard was that Jonathan mentioned there was a body in a casket at the front of the chapel. It was only about six feet away from where Janet proposed to sleep. There was to be a funeral there the next morning, so the body had already been wheeled in to await the service.

Jonathan said he could not believe his eyes.

He said, "Janet, what on earth do you think you are doing? Don't you realize there is a dead body right here next to you?"

"Of course, I realize it, Jonathan," said Janet. "But, you know something? He is a lot more *peaceful* than the man I live upstairs with. So, leave us alone, and let us get some sleep."

Janet said that before Jonathan even got to the stairs, they both started laughing, and that was the last time they had such a terrible argument. It seems that each time they started to argue, they thought about that night, and they would end up laughing.

Pastor Joe found that story highly amusing himself, thinking of Janet, barely five feet tall, and obviously unafraid of what most people would find totally disconcerting, sleeping next to a dead body.

She reminded him that, "After all, Pastor Joe, *I am* a nurse."

This made him laugh even harder, thinking of how Janet might be a nurse, but Jonathan was a funeral director, and the thought of Janet sleeping near the corpse was too eerie for Jonathan, but not for her.

Finally regaining his composure, Pastor Joe was able to talk with them about joining the church.

He was pleased with the conversation and told them he would be more than happy to present them as new members the following Sunday morning. They were happy to hear that, and eager to be a part of the church and serve the Lord in doing something in His service.

The other thing they wanted to talk with Pastor Joe about today was the possibility of their going on the mission trip to Africa that was in the process of being planned.

It was to be a four week trip into the back country in Africa. They needed Janet's nursing skills, and Jonathan wanted to accompany her, for the experience of being on a mission trip.

He had heard many stories about previous mission trips from those who spoke to the church when they returned. It seemed that things happened on those trips that were almost magical, or supernatural. He agreed with Janet that they should go, and he wanted to talk with Pastor Joe about it.

Pastor Joe was happy to hear he had two more volunteers for the trip. Since the beginning of the church, when they were in the community room, they had decided to support missions with a major portion of the church tithe. Pastor Joe and the elders of the church agreed, even after moving into the school, that they would continue to support the missions, rather than saving the money to build a larger building. They prayed about it regularly, and they were all of one accord. Pastor Joe was not going on the mission trip this time. However, about fifteen of the group that was led by Jacob Carter were going, as well as many other volunteers. Having these two young professionals along was definitely a good idea.

"Plan on it," said Pastor Joe. "We will have a meeting later this week to brief everyone on what to expect when you go on a mission trip. It won't be like being on a safari, because you won't have the luxuries provided to people who go to Africa sight-seeing. It is a rough trip, and many of our people have gotten really sick down there."

"I am not trying to talk you out of it, but it is only fair that you know what to expect. If you still want to go, then you can be at the meeting on Wednesday night here at the church. We are meeting in the youth building."

"We want to go. We feel we were called to go," said Jonathan, and Janet shook her head in agreement.

Wednesday night came, and Jonathan and Janet were among the first ones to arrive at the meeting. Jacob Carter was there, along with members of the group he had help get started. Ten of the deacons of the church were there, along with their wives, to see the presentation given by members of the congregation who had previously gone on a mission trip to Africa. Two of them were dentists, and two of them doctors. They were all willing to donate their time to help with health issues of the people in Africa, as well as to try to win souls for Christ.

After everyone was seated, Nathan Daniels took his place at the front of the group. Nathan was one of those who had been on several mission trips. He was there to share information about what the others might expect for their trip.

"Thank you all for being here this evening," he said. "You may think from the slide presentation we are showing this evening that we are trying to discourage you from going on this mission. That is far from the truth. However, the truth is what we want to show you what you will be experiencing when you take this trip."

The Power House

"If there are doubts after seeing what difficulties you may endure, or if you do not feel you are physically up to the trip, then please do not feel that you are shirking your duty to the Lord, if you decide not to go."

"There are duties involved with the mission that you could assist with, even though you might not be able to participate in the actual mission trip itself. Could we have the lights turned down, please?"

Jonathan and Janet watched, as slide after slide was shown of the African people. They were living in huts, with no running water, no electricity. These were extremely primitive conditions. Jonathan began to have some reservations about whether he would be able to endure these types of conditions.

The same feeling that caused Janet to become a nurse to care for sick people overwhelmed her once again. She knew this was a mission trip she *had* to take, regardless of the conditions they would endure. They left the meeting with mixed emotions about the trip. Jonathan was still not certain. Janet was sure that God wanted her to go, but she wanted Jonathan to be with her.

When they got home, Jonathan voiced his concerns to Janet, who, in turn, expressed her excitement and zeal for the mission.

"It isn't so much that we wouldn't have electricity or water, Janet, but look at the way the people share the common bowl. They eat with their hands. Janet, there are so many missionaries who get sick over there. Did you see the part where one man actually died from malaria?" he exclaimed. "In this day and age, it seems impossible. But, judging from the conditions the missionaries have to live in, I'm sorry, but I am just not certain I can do this."

"Then, if you aren't sure, maybe you should not go," said Janet. "But, I am going. I really want you to go, and I feel that God is calling me there to use my medical skills. In doing that, maybe there will be someone who can be won for the kingdom of God."

Janet was upset that the mission that she felt so drawn to by the Lord was becoming a subject of doubt to Jonathan. They had talked about this; he had been so sure he wanted to go. Now, it seemed as though he was not willing to be a part of it at all.

"Let's talk about it tomorrow. It's late, and I have to be at the hospital at five a.m. We will pray about it, and see what the Lord would have us do," said Janet.

"That's alright with me. I am sorry, Janet, I just don't think I can do it," said Jonathan. "But, we'll see what happens. We have until next Friday to give them our decisions on whether we are going or not."

That night, Jonathan tossed and turned until he could tell he was disturbing Janet, so he got up and went to the sofa to sleep.

As he pulled the blanket up to his chin, he thought about them sitting in Pastor Joe's office earlier that week, telling him the story about Janet sleeping on the sofa in the funeral parlor downstairs where they first lived.

He thought about how they laughed about the story, and he felt sad at the same time that he was having such negative thoughts about something that seemed so important to Janet.

He didn't fall asleep for hours, and only started dozing off as he heard Janet leaving to go to work at four thirty a.m.

The day was not much better for Jonathan, mostly due to the fact that he did not get much sleep the night before.

That night, he fell asleep and dreamed of Africa. He dreamed of smoke from fires burning around the villages, like he had seen in the films at church.

All at once, he saw a man coming through the smoke, staring at him. There was something wrong with his face. He had an ugly scar on the right side of his face, and his ear was partially gone.

As he drew nearer, Jonathan could tell that the man had been in a fire. He realized this from his years as a funeral director, having seen bodies from fires. In his dream, he saw the man coming closer, and bending down to Jonathan, who was sitting cross-legged on the ground with several other men.

He took Jonathan's face in his hands, and Jonathan heard him as he spoke to him in the African language. Although it was in African, Jonathan fully understood what the man was saying.

"Tell me about your Jesus. I need to know your Jesus," the man said to Jonathan.

Jonathan saw himself turn his face away from the man, as he struggled to stand to his feet. He tried to walk away from the man with the grotesque face. He saw himself stumble into the bushes to avoid any contact with the man. He turned and looked back.

Rather than seeing the man who had taken his face in his hands, he saw a man in white robes staring at him. Tears were running down his face. This man, too, had scars, but, his scars were in the palms of the hands that were stretched out to Jonathan, beckoning him to return. The man radiated a white light, and Jonathan put his arm up to his eyes to shield himself from the light. *He realized he was looking at his Savior.*

In his dream, Jonathan saw himself turn, and go back to the camp site, and throw himself on the ground at the man's feet. Just as Jesus placed his hand on Jonathan's head, Jonathan woke up.

The first thing he noticed when he was fully awake was that he was soaking wet from perspiration. As he went into the bathroom to change into dry pajamas, he was certain he detected a smoky odor emitting from the pajamas. The smoke odor was like it was from a campfire.

As Jonathan sensed what the odor reminded him of, he

fell to his knees and said, "Oh, Lord, forgive me, please forgive me. I will go."

Jonathan went back to the bedroom to tell Janet about his dream. He had not noticed when he got up to change his pajamas that she had already left for work. It was four forty-five in the morning. He went to the telephone and called her at the hospital, to relate the dream, and to share his decision with her.

When she came to the telephone, he said, "Janet, the most incredible thing just happened to me!"

Janet had to hold the phone away from her ear because he was speaking so loudly.

"You know I mentioned to you that one of the reasons I wanted to go on the mission trip to Africa was because of the magical or supernatural stories I have heard that came out of those trips?" he asked. "Well, I just experienced one of those happenings right here in our home while I was sleeping. Janet, I can't *wait* to go to Africa with you on this trip."

Then he told her of his dream that led to his decision.

People were staring at Janet as they passed by, seeing the joyful expression on her face. She leaned her head back and looked up at the ceiling, thanking God in her spirit that He had changed her husband's heart.

They would go, as would Jacob Carter and some members of his group. Seeing how young people in Africa lived would definitely be an impact on these young people.

The ten deacons and their wives who would go. They would witness to the older population.

Sixteen people from the choir wanted to be part of the experience. Their plans were to introduce praise and worship music to the African people in the village as their witness for Christ. They adopted, as their mission creed, *"We are the body of Christ, and, each one of us is a part of it."*

Four months after the mission trip to Africa, Pastor Joe sat in his study, reading Janet and Jonathan's latest letter.

They told him of how they almost didn't make the trip together, but how Jesus had appeared in a dream to Jonathan, beckoning him to come to Africa. Janet told about the dream in the letter, saying there was something special that Pastor Joe would read at the end.

Janet described, in great detail, an experience they had about two weeks after they arrived. She told of a tribal leader, with great influence over his people, a hero who had saved three small children by entering a burning hut to save them, being scarred on his face and body from the fire. He was a man with part of his ear missing.

She told of the man being shown to Jonathan in the dream. And how, when they made the mission trip to Africa, Jonathan was introduced to the man in the second village they visited. The man asked him to tell him the story he had heard about a man called Jesus.

The interpreter sat for hours with Jonathan and the man, so that Jonathan could witness to him and tell him the story of Jesus.

At the end of the story, the man told Jonathan, through the interpreter, that he accepted Jesus Christ as his Savior and through the witness of this tribal leader, many people in the village had, within the past few months, become followers of Christ.

Jonathan had added a postscript, telling Pastor Joe of how they had extended their trip to Africa. They would see him when they got back in two months, but it would only be a stopover. He and Janet were going to South America for a mission trip there. They had decided to become full-time missionaries.

Pastor Joe leaned back in his chair, looking out the window, and once again, laughed at the idea of tiny little Janet sleeping next to the corpse in the funeral parlor after her argument with Jonathan. Then, soberly, and prayerfully, he thanked God for the call on the lives of these two young people. He was pleased that the Lord had worked so wonderfully in their lives. He prayed it would always be so.

CHAPTER FOUR

Pastor Joe had an early meeting the next morning at the church. Eva told him she needed some time to meditate and to pray, so he gave her a goodnight kiss, and went upstairs to bed.

Eva had just sat down and opened her Bible, when the telephone rang. It was Grace Stuart, one of the members of their church.

She asked Eva if she would come to the hospital. Grace said she had been admitted that afternoon and needed to talk to someone. Eva asked if she would like Pastor Joe to come with her, but Grace hesitated, then told Eva she would rather she come alone.

Eva told her she would be there as soon as she could get dressed. She went upstairs and told her husband about the telephone call, and where she was going.

"What is wrong, Eva?" Pastor Joe asked, with the concern he always showed for one of his flock.

"Joe, I really don't know. All Grace said is that she desperately needs someone to talk with right away, so I told her I would come."

"Well, be careful driving over there. I pray that God will meet her needs. Wake me when you come in, so I will know you got home safely."

Fifteen minutes later, Eva walked down the corridor of the hospital to Grace's room. She knew Grace as a reverent and quiet lady who came to the altar frequently, and had often asked for prayer for her daughter, Tina.

She barely recognized her when she saw her lying in the hospital bed. Grace had lost so much weight, and there were dark circles beneath her eyes. She looked as though she had aged twenty years. Eva forced a smile when she saw Grace.

"Thank you for coming to see me, Mrs. DuPriest," Grace said, taking the hand that Eva offered. "I'm sorry to call you so late. Oh, I know I must look terrible."

"Oh, no, it's Eva, honey, just call me Eva. And, there's no need to apologize. I would have come sooner, if I had known you were here. Now, please tell me, Grace. What is wrong?"

"Oh, Eva, I need you to pray with me about something."

Then, she began to tell Eva the entire story that led up to the reason she was in the hospital.

Grace was a single mother whose husband had been killed in a work related accident at the local boat factory. She had raised her young daughter, Tina, from the age of five, by herself.

Grace worked as a court reporter. She made enough money to support herself and Tina, but they did not live extravagant lives. She had received payment from a small insurance policy when her husband, Greg, was killed. That money was put away for Tina's education.

When Tina became fifteen, she got in with the wrong crowd. She began wearing clothes that were much too old for her. When Grace refused to buy the kind of clothes Tina wanted to wear, she borrowed or traded clothes with her friends. She started wearing heavy makeup, and began wanting to stay out later and later.

Grace told Eva that the conversations between she and her daughter usually were limited to the words, "No!" and

"Well, why not, everybody else does." It made her sad, but it seemed she couldn't do anything to convince Tina that she was headed in the wrong direction. They had always attended church together. Now, it was all she could do to get Tina to go once a month.

Grace told Eva that she *had* to work. She worked demanding hours, having a tight schedule to get her notes typed up and back to court on time. Sometimes she brought her work home with her. She would get home about the time Tina would get in from school, just so she could keep an eye on her.

At sixteen, Tina was totally out of control. There were fights between herself and her mother. She argued with her teachers. She was constantly in fights with the kids at school. She refused to go to church with Grace anymore. She stayed out way past her curfew of twelve-thirty. Grace felt like all she did was tell Tina she was grounded. It was to no avail.

A well-meaning friend suggested to Grace that she and Tina see a spiritual counselor she knew. Grace assumed he was a Christian counselor.

She told Eva, in detail, about the day they went to see Mr. Brooks.

They had gone up the walk to an old antebellum house that was greatly in need of repair. The front room had been made into a reception room. A tall, thin, and totally disinterested girl sat at a desk, polishing her fingernails a bright purple. She had them sign in and led them to a room in the back of the house.

When she pulled back the curtain that covered the door, Grace noticed there were cushions on the floor, rather than chairs. The scent of incense permeated the room. There was no other place to sit, so she and Tina took a seat on the floor cushions.

She had an eerie feeling about the whole thing and immediately felt the urge to leave. But Tina said, "Cool", looking around at the various types of candles burning around the room. This was the first positive sign Tina had shown about the idea of counseling, so Grace decided to see what the spiritual counselor would be like. She found out in short order.

Mr. Brooks seemed to float into the room, wearing a flowing muslin robe and sandals. Grace's feelings were confirmed. This was definitely not what she expected, and she wanted to get up and leave. Mr. Brooks looked completely stoned. He had glanced at Grace and Tina on the way to a cushion and waved his hand in the air.

"And so it begins," he said. "The age old struggle between mother and daughter. Ahhh," he sighed, as he sunk down on a cushion. "Let's begin."

He addressed his remarks to Tina, rather than Grace.

"My dear, pray tell me how all this maternal smothering is affecting you at your tender age of sixteen years?"

Tina looked at her mother and smiled, almost certain she and Mr. Brooks were on the same wave length. They were both against her mother. She was correct.

Grace found herself feeling as though she were on trial in that room. She tried to explain to Mr. Brooks her feeling that her daughter was out of control. That she rebelled against all authority from her mother. That Tina showed no respect for her or any other adult. She told him about how Tina wanted to do body piercing and tattoos. Grace told him this was something she did not approve of her daughter doing, at sixteen years old.

His comment to her was, "Well, she may decide at some point to want a full body tattoo, and compliment it with green hair, but that is part of the mystique of teenage years, isn't it? Besides, what do you care? It's *her* body."

At that point, Grace picked her purse up from the floor beside her and grabbed Tina's hand.

"Let's go, Tina," she said.

As they exited through the curtain, Tina was laughing hysterically over what Mr. Brooks had said. Grace looked back in time to see Mr. Brooks lighting a strange looking contraption that she later heard was probably a water pipe. All she knew at the time was that she couldn't get out of that house fast enough.

When they got to the car, Tina was still laughing, and looked at her mother and said, "Man, Mr. Brooks is the bomb! That was way too sweet! Wait until I tell Connie and the others! And to think, Mom, this was all *your* idea."

Grace was humiliated beyond words. She said nothing on the way home. Tina would stop laughing, then, start again every time she thought of what Mr. Brooks had said. And to think, he said it to her straight-laced, Christian mother. The recollection of the look on her mother's face was just too much. She couldn't help but laugh.

The situation had been anything but funny to Grace. She had taken the afternoon off, without pay, to try to seek help for the relationship between herself and her daughter. It certainly had not turned out as she had hoped.

She began to question whether she really knew the friend that had suggested they see Mr. Brooks. She thought Rita knew her better than to send her to someone like that.

Eva could hear the hurt in her voice as Grace related the entire story to her.

She sat quietly, listening to Grace finish her story.

The situation with Tina continued to deteriorate. One afternoon, when Tina was eighteen, Grace was sitting at her desk at the courthouse, waiting to do her court reporting duties for a trial that was to begin in half an hour. She looked up to see Connie, Tina's best friend. Connie looked unsure as to whether to come into Grace's office. Grace went out into the hallway and led her into her office.

"Hi there, Connie. What are you doing here at this time of day? Why aren't you in school?"

This was the first semester of college for Tina and Connie. They were lucky to live in a college town, so Tina could continue to live at home and save that much in expenses. Otherwise, she probably would not have been able to go. She certainly couldn't have gotten a scholarship with the grade point average she had. Grace knew that both Tina and Connie were supposed to be in class right then.

"I came by to see you," said Connie. "There's something you need to know. It's about Tina."

"Why? What's the matter, Connie?" asked Grace, anxiously, coming back from around her desk where she had been about to sit. "Is she alright?" she asked, taking Connie by the shoulders.

"Well, I am afraid she is in some big trouble," said Connie. "There is this girl, Brandi, that doesn't like Tina a bit. Tina is going with Mike, the guy Brandi used to date, and Brandi still likes him. He dumped her, she didn't dump him. Anyhow, Tina backed into her car the other day. She told me it was an accident, but you know how Tina is when she is mad."

"Unfortunately, I do," said Grace. "Oh no, we don't have insurance on her anymore, either, because we got cancelled last month. Whose car was she driving? It couldn't have been mine. I have had it all week."

"Well, she was in Mike's car, and he doesn't have insurance either, because he lost his license two months ago from too many speeding tickets."

"Here's the thing, Mrs. Stuart. Brandi told Tina that she would let her out of having to pay to get the fender fixed, if Tina would go to a certain house and pick up a package for her and put it in Brandi's refrigerator at her dorm, no questions asked."

"Oh, no!" said Grace, putting her hand over her mouth.

"Oh, yes," said Connie. "I tried to get her not to do it. But, you know Tina. She was afraid that Brandi, or her parents, would call you and ask for the money to fix her car.

So, she did it. She used Mike's car and went to this guy's house and picked up the package. She was trying to get Brandi's door open with the key Brandi gave her when the police busted her."

"Busted her?"

"Yeah, you know, it was all a set-up. Brandi had tipped them off that Tina was going to be coming on the school grounds with dope. She told this wild story that Tina was on drugs, that she had crashed Brandi's car. She told the policeman that she overheard Tina telling someone that she was planning on setting Brandi up by putting drugs in Brandi's refrigerator at the dorm. She said she heard Tina saying she went in Brandi's room when her room mate was there and took Brandi's extra key. They were waiting on her when she got back from picking up the package for Brandi."

"Oh, dear Lord, no," said Grace, looking horrified. "Where is she?"

"They took her down to the police station. I left the school as soon as they did, to come tell you. I figure you will be getting a call any minute."

A thought occurred to Grace.

"Connie, you have got to tell me the truth. Does Tina use drugs?"

"Not that I know of, Mrs. Stuart. Neither one of us do. We have been to some parties where there was some real doping going on and those people got too weird and screwed up. Scared both of us into *not* doing it. We have smoked, but just cigarettes. Oh, yeah, and we did try some peach brandy once in high school. It made Tina real sick. She tried it one morning before breakfast. Some guy gave it to her in a Coke can. I took a sip of it, but it tasted like peach gasoline to me. But, Tina liked the taste of it and drank it too fast. She ended up throwing up in the trash can in the study hall in front of everybody. It was *not* a pretty sight," said Connie, wrinkling her brow and scratching the side of her

The Power House

head as she recalled the incident.

Grace stood in a trancelike state, as she stood there listening to Connie recapitulating the things in which Connie and her daughter had gotten involved. She couldn't believe it had all gotten so out of hand. She closed her eyes, wishing Connie would go away. She didn't want to hear anymore. About that time, the telephone rang. She just stood for a few seconds, staring at the phone.

She finally grabbed the phone and answered, "Good afternoon, Court Reporting."

The voice on the other end of the phone said, "May I speak with Mrs. Grace Stuart, please?"

"Speaking," said Grace.

"This is Sergeant Gray from down at police headquarters on Main Street. We have your daughter Tina here. Can you please come down right away?"

"I'm on my way," said Grace.

Grace hung up the telephone, then, turned to Connie.

"Thank you, Connie, for coming all the way down here to tell me what happened with Tina. Let me drop you back at school on the way. I don't want you to get in trouble, too."

"No problem," said Connie. "Cindy is outside waiting on me. She will take me back. Tell Tina I am sorry. I will call her later. If worse comes to worse, have her call me when she can."

Grace gathered her things to leave. She asked Roberta, the other court reporter, to cover for her that afternoon. She left for the police station to see what she could do for her daughter. Her heart was heavy.

She looked up at the sky and said, "Oh, Greg, why did you have to die? I need you so badly right now. Things would never have turned out like this if you hadn't died!"

She began to cry, then, realized she would need to keep her wits about her, if she was going to be able to help her daughter.

"Please, God help us, please help us," she prayed as she entered the police station.

When they brought Tina out, she didn't look like the rebellious teenager that had left for school that morning. She looked like the little five year old girl with the great big blue eyes that Grace had picked up at her father's funeral and hugged because she didn't understand what was happening. Grace wanted to hug her daughter and tell her she was there for her, but they kept her on another side of the desk, as they talked with Grace about Tina's charges.

Tina was charged with possession with intent to deliver. The package she had picked up had contained heroin. It was a large amount.

"The good news is that she passed her drug test. It's a good thing we didn't have to tack using charges onto those she has now," said Sergeant Gray. "Still, as it is, she stands the risk of going to jail for a long time, if convicted."

Grace could not believe she was hearing this. It was like a bad dream. She shook her head to clear her senses, but this was real. This was truly happening. She told Tina that she knew most of the attorneys from working in the courthouse. She would get a good attorney for her.

The police sergeant looked at Grace and said, solemnly, "You had better. She is going to need it."

Finally, he left the room and let Grace talk to Tina alone, but they had to sit across from one another, with no physical contact. Crying and extremely distraught, Tina told Grace the same story Connie had. It looked like a set-up, but how on earth could they prove it? Only time would tell.

Eva sat quietly listening to Grace's story. She knew she could do the most good for Grace just by letting her finish her story. Her heart went out to her.

"Go ahead, Grace. Tell me what happened."

Grace continued her story.

The day of the trial arrived. Grace had lost about twenty

pounds since the day they took her only child to jail. Tina was thin to begin with, but looked like a waif when they brought her into the courtroom. Because of the amount of heroin she had in her possession when they caught her, and the fact that Grace worked and couldn't be home with Tina, they kept her in jail until the trial. She had been there for six weeks.

Grace had wanted to get Trent Jones to represent Tina. He was reputed to be one of the best criminal attorneys in the state. However, Trent was tied up in a big criminal case that would last for months. Everyone else she talked to had cases scheduled. She had to settle for an attorney who had never tried a case like this one.

Ralph Gleason had only been practicing for a year. He was the best they could do.

Grace didn't have a good feeling about it from the beginning. All she could do was pray that God would help them. It seemed she was praying constantly these days.

One particular morning, she prayed in the car on the way to her job at the courthouse.

She was asking God, "Why is all this happening, Lord? What else could I have done for Tina so she would have listened to me? Why can't I get a good attorney for my child, when it feels like it's a life and death situation to me right now? Lord, why, oh why does everything seem so hopeless? I do love you, Lord, and I trust you. We need your help so badly."

At the very moment she stopped praying that morning, the Lord spoke to Grace's spirit. He gave her a word meant just for her. The meaning was profound. She reached over to scribble across the steno pad she carried in case she had to take notes at a moment's notice for one of the attorneys.

She wrote the words as the Lord had told them to her with His assurance:

"The Lord's purpose in this adversity is greater than your comfort in the situation."

She didn't have any idea what the Lord's purpose in this could possibly be, but she acknowledged that the situation was anything but comfortable.

The trial lasted for two consecutive days. There was no jury. There was only a judge. Judge Parks seemed sympathetic to Tina, speaking kindly to her when he asked her to repeat an answer.

Brandi testified that she knew nothing about the drugs, but that Tina had been trying to set her up by stealing her room key and had planned to plant them there. She accused Tina of damaging her car by intentionally backing into it. Some of her friends were there to substantiate her story.

Connie and some other friends testified for Tina, claiming it was all a scheme of revenge concocted by Brandi. They indicated that it was a true case of Brandi believing the old adage *"all is fair in love and war."* This had to do with love. But, Brandi had declared war on Tina for taking her boyfriend away from her.

Grace had talked with other attorneys and they told her that all Ralph Gleason, Tina's attorney, needed to do was plead entrapment. Grace talked to Ralph, and he agreed that would be exactly what he would do. He got so nervous during the trial, however, he somehow forgot that part, and he never mentioned a word about entrapment.

Grace was not allowed to sit with Ralph and Tina. She sat in the courtroom with the others involved in the case. In her mind, she was screaming at Ralph to bring up the idea of entrapment. He was aware of the seriousness of the charges, but he was inexperienced in this type of case. He fumbled and stumbled his way through it.

Tina was convicted and given a sentence of twenty years because of the amount of drugs involved, and because it came down to her word against Brandi's. The sentence might even have been stiffer if Tina hadn't been only eighteen. After all, she was caught red-handed with the drugs, seemingly trying to plant them in Brandi's room.

Tina would have to serve a number of years before she would be considered for parole. She would be sent to a jail in the same state they lived, but Grace could see her only once a month. She would have to wait until after the first three months even to do that. Grace sat in the courtroom, stunned, when the verdict was passed down.

Tina did not take her eyes off her mother. She saw the toll this had taken on Grace, from the additional grey in her hair, and the lines on her face. She was fearful for her mother's health and what would happen to her now. She felt extremely sorry for what she was putting her through. And, she was very frightened for herself, as well.

They allowed Tina to say goodbye to her mother. As she stood hugging her daughter, tears flowing down her face, she heard someone say, "It's time, Mrs. Stuart."

She let go of Tina, who was trying to be brave for her mother and not cry. Grace turned to look at the man who had spoken to her.

When she looked around, two policewomen were roughly pulling her daughter's hands together to put handcuffs on her. The other was starting to put shackles on Tina's feet. Tina looked like a frightened child beside these huge, uniformed women.

The sight of her beautiful little girl being shackled at her feet, like a hardened criminal, tore through Grace like a knife in her heart. Grace heard the sound of screaming, becoming louder and louder. She did not realize it was her own.

That was the last thing she remembered.

The next thing she knew, Grace was looking into the concerned face of three paramedics. They were poised over her with a defibrillator, waiting to discharge it into her chest. One was holding her arm, trying to find a pulse. One was pushing on her chest and the other trying to administer oxygen to her.

The Power House

She sat up enough to see that her jacket had been cut off her in order to get the equipment to her body to revive her.

It took a few moments for her to remember where she was. She saw Tina trying to pull away from the policewomen to reach her mother, a frantic look on her face. When Grace remembered where she was, and why, she lost consciousness once again.

The next day, she woke up in the hospital, only to remember where her child must be right then. She began to cry hysterically, and began pulling at the wires on the equipment that was connected to her.

That caused her monitor to malfunction, and a nurse came in immediately. The nurse adjusted the monitor, and noting Grace's emotional state, asked her if she would like her to call someone for her. Grace told her that she didn't want to call anyone.

She had not said anything to Eva or Pastor Joe about the situation because she was so ashamed.

She told Eva that, as she was praying that evening, she realized that now was not the time to be proud. She needed someone who would pray with her for her child. She might even be dying herself, so she needed someone to pray for her, as well.

She did not know Eva personally, but had spoken to her after church nearly every Sunday as Eva stood beside Pastor Joe, as the people in the congregation exited.

After Grace had told Eva the entire story of what had happened to her daughter, she said, "Oh, Eva, I need you to pray with me."

With tears in her own eyes, Eva said, "Give me your hand, Grace, and we will pray."

"Our Dear all- knowing and all- powerful Lord. I pray that you would comfort my dear sister Grace in her time of sorrow. This situation is so hard, Lord. We pray for mercy for Tina. We ask in the name of Jesus that you show her mercy. Nothing is too difficult for you, Lord. Help us find a way to help Tina. We know with you all things are possible. You gave Grace a word, Father. We stand on your word Lord. We will trust in you with all our hearts, leaning not to our own understanding. We will, in all our ways, acknowledge you, and you will make straight our path."

"Lord, I pray that you would be with Grace during this difficult time. Help her to regain her physical strength, Father. Please help her know she can depend on your love and your comfort. In Jesus name I pray these things, Amen."

Eva stayed with Grace until the nurses came and told her the doctor would be coming in to make his rounds and all visitors were being asked to leave. Grace thanked Eva as she gathered her purse and coat to leave.

"I will be back in the morning, Grace. Pastor Joe and I will be praying for you. If it is alright with you, we have a prayer chain that would be more than glad to pray for you and Tina. I can call the first person on the chain when I get home."

"Thank you, Eva. Yes, please, the more prayers we can get, the better."

Eva smiled and patted Grace on the shoulder.

"See you in the morning," she said.

Two weeks after she was released from the hospital, Grace came back to church. Eva made a point of trying to speak to Grace after church, even if she had to cut her conversation with others short. Some knew what had happened, those on the prayer chain. Some did not know.

Grace continued to go to the altar to pray for Tina. Many times, Eva would go and kneel beside her and pray with her for mercy for Grace's child. She knew in her heart it would take a miracle from God to change things.

Then, a miracle happened.

The first part of the miracle was that the case Trent Jones was working on was suddenly settled out of court, and Trent was free to help Grace. He had felt bad about the way the verdict had come out, knowing it might have gone the other way, if only he had been free at the time to represent Tina.

He went immediately to Grace and told her he was going to file an appeal. He would be there to represent Tina this time.

Grace felt some relief, but even though she knew there would be an appeal, she couldn't imagine how Trent would be able to convince the judge, when he had said all the evidence was against Tina. She called Pastor Joe and Eva and asked them to begin to pray with all their might.

CHAPTER FIVE

Trent Jones had earned the reputation of being one of the toughest attorneys in the state. He had been working in the legal system for twenty years, and he knew the law. He also knew that Ralph Gleason should have pleaded entrapment during the first trial. But, since he did not, there would have to be more to the case, this time, in order to prove Tina's innocence.

Trent Jones started an investigation, and it didn't take long for him to uncover evidence that he felt would turn the case around. He kept most of the information between himself and his partner, knowing how word gets around. That could have destroyed his case for Tina.

The day of the new trial arrived. Trent Jones asked the judge to make note that Tina was poorly represented in the previous trial and the attorney representing her should have pleaded entrapment. He went so far as to mention that the previous trial had been a travesty of justice.

Trent was confident that he would be able to reverse the verdict. He had done a thorough job in preparing for this trial.

He called Tina to testify as to what happened, along with Connie and her other friends who had testified previously.

He called Brandi to testify, as well the people who testified in her behalf at the original trial.

Pastor Joe and Eva were in the court room with Grace to hear the testimonies. They knew the whole story up until now, and they wanted to be there to support Grace.

The judge was the same judge who heard the case previously. As Judge Parks listened to the testimonies, he was constantly tapping his pen on the desk. Trent had been in the courtroom with Judge Parks presiding many times. He knew the pen tapping meant the judge was impatient and didn't think he was hearing anything new. It was as though he was frustrated and impatient with having to sit through the same thing all over again. Trent knew that meant the same verdict, if he couldn't do better than the last attorney had done.

He knew now was the time to call his key witness. One who had not testified at the original trial, one that nobody expected. Mike Sellars, the former boyfriend of Brandi, supposedly the current boyfriend of Tina Stuart. Mike had been subpoenaed for the original trial; however, Ralph Gleason never called him. Trent Jones had discovered that fact, after carefully reviewing the notes from the previous trial.

What Mike had to say would shock the entire courtroom, including Tina herself, who thought she knew Mike well.

"I want to beg the court's indulgence in hearing Mr. Sellars' entire story. Each thing he is going to tell is relevant to the reason why he is here today," said Trent.

He then turned to address Mike, who had just finished taking his oath. The judge interrupted him.

"First, I would like you to tell the court why you *have* decided to come forth with your testimony today, Mr. Sellars. And, please tell the court why you didn't come forth for the original trial," said Judge Parks.

"I was never called to testify, Your Honor. I was in the

courtroom every day of the original trial, but I didn't come forward at the time, because they never called me to testify, and I didn't want to at the time. But, I am here today because of that lady right there, Your Honor. Grandmother Sellars," said Mike.

He nodded at his grandmother, who was sitting on the front row in the courtroom. He gave her a half smile, then, turned back to the judge.

"Continue with your story," said Judge Parks.

"One night I had been out smoking pot with some of my friends. I have had asthma since I was just a kid. I usually don't have much of a problem with it. That night, I guess I overdid it on smoking. The weed was kind of rough, but that's all Jimmy had, so we smoked it."

He stopped, nervously clearing his throat.

"Anyway, on the way home, I got to where I was having trouble breathing. By the time I came in through the kitchen, I was really bad off. I had hoped I could get upstairs to get my inhaler, but when I started up the back steps into the kitchen, I knew I couldn't make it. My lungs were almost closed at that point."

"Thank God that Grandmother Sellars was sitting in the kitchen, drinking her tea right then. Everyone else had gone to bed. But, there was Grandmother, waiting on me to come home like she always does. I didn't know she waited up on me every night, until that night. She told me she had always waited up for me. Anyway, I could hardly breathe. So, she went upstairs and got my inhaler and brought it down to me, where I was sitting on the floor of the kitchen against the wall. She actually got down there on the floor with me and had me lie down with my head in her lap, after I used my inhaler. Then, she started to pray for me."

"After about fifteen minutes, I was breathing okay again. It really scared me, what had just happened. Grandmother and I sat on the floor for over two hours. I finally broke down and told her that I am a junkie. A no- good, dope smoking, heroin addict. It really wasn't any news to her, she had suspected all along. She knew I was lying to her when I denied using drugs. She and my parents tried to talk to me about how drugs are bad, not to mention illegal."

He glanced nervously at the judge when he said the part about *illegal.*

His voice broke when he began talking again.

"My grandmother has been praying for me since I was a little kid. I went to church with her quite a bit when I was a kid, but I quit going when I was about eleven. But, you know, she never gave up on me. I would see her sitting in her room, doing her cross-stitch, and she would just stop and bow her head and pray that God would watch out over me. I never thought anything about it, except that it was kind of sweet. That night on the kitchen floor, I realized I could have died, and while I was trying to breathe, I looked up into my grandmother's face and knew who really loved me."

Mike began to cry.

"After she heard all I had to tell her about the drugs, she told me about Jesus. She reminded me that He died for my sins. She told me that taking drugs was wrong, that my body was the temple of the Lord. She told me that the Lord would forgive me, if I sincerely asked Him to."

"She talked to me for an hour about how she had been praying He would turn me around, before it was too late."

"I really listened, for the first time, to every word she said, and all of a sudden, I saw myself as Jesus must have been seeing me. I was sitting there on the floor, wasted on dope and lying on my grandmother's lap, with her praying for Him to save me."

"It made me sick to see myself through His eyes. I gave my life to Him, there on the kitchen floor, in my grandmother's arms. I am sorry for what I did, but I hope I can help repair some of the damage by my testimony today. I know that is what Jesus would have me do."

Mike wiped the tears from his eyes with the back of his hand. He looked up to see his grandmother blowing her nose from crying, hearing the testimony her grandson was giving for the Lord, right in the courtroom.

Grace herself was crying, and she could see that the judge was swallowing hard.

"Tina shouldn't be in jail," said Mike. "The whole thing was set up by Brandi. I know, because I was part of the set-up."

Tina and Grace turned to look at one another, with mouths open in astonishment at what Mike was saying. Pastor Joe squeezed Eva's hand. They all waited to see what Mike had to tell the court.

"Brandi and I had got together a couple of days before this thing happened. We went and did some *H* together. We spent the night at her Aunt Bonnie's place. Her aunt was out of town on business and Brandi had a key. Brandi had a camcorder and set it in the corner, so it would record us doing the drugs. I didn't think much about the camcorder, because I was in a hurry to do the drugs."

He shifted uncomfortably in his seat, glancing over at Brandi.

If looks could kill, Mike would have fallen off the witness chair from the one Brandi was giving him at the moment. That did not escape notice of Judge Parks, either.

"Anyhow, Brandi had this way of being able to get the best drugs. I asked her how, and she told me that she would share the information about that, and the drugs if we could get back together. I agreed to do it."

Mike asked for a drink of water. The judge nodded his permission for the bailiff to bring him a glass. Mike took a sip of water, then, choked on it. He avoided looking at Tina.

"I'm sorry, Your Honor. I'm just real nervous right now."

He finished taking a long drink of water, then, resumed

his testimony.

"Well, Brandi and I got really high that night. She decided things were getting boring, so she wanted to have some fun with Tina. I figured that since I was going to be dropping her anyway, what the heck, you know?"

He looked down, refusing to look in Tina's direction. Then, he stared straight ahead, remembering the plan Brandi had come up with to get even with Tina.

"Brandi told me that she could get a certain quantity of *H* from her source."

"Tell the court what you mean by *H*, Mike," interrupted Trent Jones.

"Uh, heroin, sir."

"You said in your last statement that Brandi told you she could get a certain quantity of heroin from her source. Is that correct?" asked Trent.

"Yes, sir."

"Tell us who that source is, Mike."

"Well, yes sir. It's, uh, it's him."

Mike pointed to Bobby Parish, the arresting officer in the case.

Bobby Parish had been sitting in the courtroom, in the event he was called to testify. He looked straight at Mike, in total disbelief of what Mike was saying.

Everyone in the courtroom gasped at what Mike had just revealed to the court.

"I object! That's hearsay!" shouted Dan Stanley, the prosecuting attorney.

"Your Honor, please permit the witness to continue. If he is allowed to finish his statement, the court will see that what he is telling is much more than hearsay," Trent Jones argued.

"Overruled," said Judge Parks. "Continue, son".

Judge Parks had heard from quite a few sources there had been evidence disappearing from the crime lab in many of the drug cases. He wanted to hear what information Mike

The Power House

might have, to see if there was hard evidence to indicate Bobby Parish.

"Well, it turns out she was telling the truth about that part, at least. What Bobby didn't know when he brought Brandi some dope to her aunt's house that night is, that I was in the coat closet in the foyer."

"And, he also didn't know that the video camera was still on from where we had been doing the dope and all. It's all right there on that video tape."

He indicated a tape that was lying on the table in front of Trent Jones.

This time, Bobby Parish looked panicked. He turned to look at Brandi.

She turned her head away from him, refusing to return his accusing stare.

Mike continued with his testimony.

"Brandi had told me that Bobby Parish was getting drugs from the police evidence room. Brandi would get a stash from him, keep enough for herself, and then sell the rest on the street, and give him the money. All she wanted was the drugs, and all he wanted was the money. It was a sweet deal for both of them. I guess I thought it was for me, too, because she was willing to share her drugs with me."

"Continue with your story about the set-up, Mike," said Trent Jones, as Mike paused to take a deep breath.

"Well, like I said, Brandi and I were real high. She wanted to get even for Tina being with me, so she said it would prove I really loved her if I would go along with it."

"At that point, I cared more about the drugs than I did about Tina, or Brandi, so I just said, "Yeah, whatever."

Grace looked at her daughter, sensing the humiliation she must be feeling at the way Mike was talking about her. And, about the part he admitted he played in setting her up. Tina looked at Mike, tears forming in her eyes, as she surveyed her Judas.

Mike still refused to look at Tina. He began to speak again.

"Well, she said she was going to make Tina mad so she would do something stupid to retaliate against her. That would be the first part that would start making people believe Brandi's story she was concocting."

"So, she really made Tina mad, walking by in the hall after class and giving me a kiss right in front of Tina and saying, "Ooooh, Mikey, that kiss is better than the one you gave me last night."

"Then, she ran out to her car. Tina had my car keys, so she took off after Brandi. She got in my car, and backed into Brandi's car while Brandi was backing out, trying to block her from driving off. She bent Brandi's fender pretty bad. That was what Brandi had been waiting for. To everyone watching, it looked like it was Tina's fault out there in the parking lot and that Tina was out to get Brandi."

"Then the next day, Brandi got the heroin from Bobby. She convinced Tina that she was going to work a deal with her to let her out of having to pay for fixing the car, because she knew Tina and her mom didn't have much money."

"She told Tina she would let her out of fixing the car, if she would go to this guy's house and pick up something for her. She gave her a key to her dorm room and told her that, after she got the stuff, to put it in her refrigerator."

"Then Brandi told her wild story and got everybody believing what she said, that Tina was trying to set her up. But, it was really the other way around."

"It was no coincidence that the arresting officer was Bobby Parish."

There was total silence in the courtroom as Mike Sellars finished his testimony.

Dan Stanley, the prosecutor, was extremely careful in his cross-examination of Mike, but was not able to get him to recant any portion of the testimony. That testimony

The Power House

included the fact that Mike was involved.

Mr. Stanley asked if Mike had been informed that he might be charged for his involvement in the set-up. Mike stood on his testimony, even though he realized he might suffer legal consequences from his involvement in what happened.

Mike said, "The only thing they talked to me about was obstruction of justice. I admit it was wrong to do what we did to Tina. I'm sorry I went along with Brandi, and I have promised my grandmother I would go to rehab as soon as this trial is over."

The next witness was Donnie Black, the young man that Brandi had talked into giving the package to Tina when she stopped by his house.

He told the court he knew nothing of the contents of the package and nothing of the plan for setting up Tina.

Brandi had promised to go out with him, if he would do that one thing for her, and that was his only reason for being involved. He said he would take a lie-detector test to prove he was telling the truth.

Judge Parks ordered the video to be played. The video showed exactly what Mike Sellars had testified happened. It showed Brandi and Mike shooting heroin in their veins. It showed Bobby Parish coming to the door, and Mike quickly hiding in the coat closet in the foyer. It showed Brandi opening the door for Bobby and him coming inside. It showed him handing her the drugs.

In full view of the camera, Bobby Parish opened the package and showed the drugs to Brandi and told her how much the stuff was worth on the street.

At that point, Brandi invited Bobby to stay, but he told her he was in a hurry. He said he was on duty and had to get back to the station.

After Bobby left, Brandi told her plan to Mike about setting Tina up. The tape showed Mike agreeing to go along with it.

"From now on, we *have* to be best friends. We both know too much," she laughed wickedly, in full view of the camera.

Mike told the court that at the end of the evening, she copied the tape and gave him a copy. When she handed it to him, she suggested that he keep his copy of the tape and play it if he ever had second thoughts about dropping her again. She reminded him that she was keeping the original, and that she would always have the "goods" on him. She said it in a teasing manner, but they both knew she was serious about her threat.

At that point, Judge Parks said, "I have heard enough. Turn off the video. Mark it as evidence. Release Miss Stuart. I reverse the order of the court. She is not guilty."

He tapped his gavel and stood up. The others in the courtroom rose. He turned to the bailiff, then, pointed to Bobby Parish.

"I want Sergeant Parish arrested and charged. Cuff him and read him his rights. And I want it done before anybody leaves this room."

He looked at Brandi, and said, "The policeman here will read you your rights."

"The same goes for you, Mr. Sellars. I applaud your decision to come forth and tell the truth, however, there may be consequences, due to your involvement with obstruction of justice. Do you understand?"

Mike Sellars held his head high and looked directly at the judge.

"I knew when I came in to tell my story there probably would be some sort of consequences. I am ready to do the right thing, your Honor, even if I have to spend time in jail."

"Then, I hereby declare that court's adjourned," said Judge Parks.

Grace jumped out of her seat in the courtroom and ran to her daughter, Tina, who met her halfway up the aisle.

"Oh, thank God, Mama," she cried, as she reached her mother, throwing herself in her mother's outstretched arms.

She was so relieved that this nightmare was over. The only thing she wanted was to do was go home and lock the world outside her door.

What a difficult lesson for such a young girl. What a traumatic toll it had taken on her mother, as well.

Pastor Joe and Eva were there to hug Tina and congratulate her on the findings, as soon as she stopped hugging her mother.

Tina had spent many hours alone in her jail cell during the past several months. She told Pastor Joe and Eva that, during her time in jail, she had started to pray, asking God to help her. She had begun to trust in Him, as she had as a small child. More than once, in the middle of the dark of night, she had called on Jesus to help her, and He had comforted her with His word.

There was one thing Tina felt strongly compelled to do before she left the courtroom that day. She excused herself from talking with Pastor Joe and Eva, and walked slowly to the front where Mike Sellars stood with a deputy, who was reading him his rights. He looked up as Tina approached.

Tina waited until the deputy finished speaking.

"Mike, I want to thank you for coming here today and telling the court what happened. I know it wasn't an easy thing to do. Especially knowing they would be playing that tape and that your grandmother would have to see it. It took a lot of courage, and I want you to know that I appreciate it more than you could know," she said.

Mike listened to what Tina had to say. He had his head down, and at first, couldn't look her in the eye.

Then, he looked up at her and said, "Tina, I am so sorry for what we put you through. There is no way you should have had to spend that time in jail. And, I see what it has done to you and your mom. I just pray you will find it in your heart to forgive me some day."

"Well, Mike, after what you just did, consider today that day. I do forgive you."

She kissed her fingertips, then, placed them on Mike's cheek.

"And may God bless you and help you through rehab," she added.

"God bless you, too, Tina," Mike answered.

She turned to leave and found herself face to face with Mike's grandmother, who had walked up in time to hear the conversation between Mike and Tina.

His grandmother reached out and hugged her. She had always liked Tina. She felt sorry for what had happened to her, and that her grandson had been involved. Tina cried and hugged her back.

"Bless you, Mrs. Sellars, for leading Mike to Jesus. I don't think any of this today would have ever happened, if it hadn't been for you."

Mrs. Sellars stepped back and said, "With God, all things are possible, Tina. Remember that."

Tina returned to where her mother stood with Pastor Joe and Eva. She went to her mother, and they left the courtroom arm in arm.

That first night home, Grace and Tina talked until dawn the next morning. The telephone rang five different times, however, neither of them wanted to talk to anyone in the world other than one another.

Tina shared with Grace the horror of being locked away in a jail cell, knowing she was innocent of what she had been convicted.

She told Grace how she had started to pray again, to ask Jesus to come back into her heart. How she had prayed for her mother every day and every night.

Grace had given her a Bible to keep in the jail cell. Tina shared with her mother about how the Lord would lead her to the passages in His word that gave her comfort in the middle of the night.

Grace was finally able to share with Tina about her own reliance on the Lord for strength, and have Tina understand what she meant. She shared with her about the word the Lord had given her that day in the car.

"The Lord's purpose in this adversity is greater than your comfort in the situation."

Tina and Grace both had a good idea, now, of what God had been trying to say that day. It was His Blessed assurance, from heaven above.

For the first time since she was a small child, Tina and her mother held hands and thanked God, together, for His goodness and His mercy. They both cried like babies. They discovered that hugs and tears help heal broken hearts.

After Tina returned home, she stayed out of school for the rest of that semester, and the one that followed. She got a job working at the mall in one of the department stores and paid her mother back for the money she had spent on the attorney fees for her case.

Grace tried to get her to save the money; however, Tina insisted that it was time for her to take responsibility for herself and her actions.

This was one of Tina's first steps in becoming a mature woman. Grace was proud of her daughter for doing the right thing, for the first time in many years.

When the next semester began, Tina started back to school. She changed her major, and began to come home after classes. The lesson Tina learned had been difficult for both her and her mother, but what came from their trials was a new life for Tina and a newfound bond between mother and daughter.

After sharing the experience of what had happened with Tina, Grace and Eva had become close friends. Grace often came over to have coffee with Eva on Saturday mornings.

The Power House

This morning, they were talking about how things had gotten so much better with Grace and Tina's relationship.

"*The Lord's purpose in this adversity,*" mused Eva, as Grace shared the news with her about Tina's starting college.

The Lord had known all along what it would take to turn Tina around. She was so strong headed that it took something tragic like what happened to bring her back to Him.

After Grace left that morning, Pastor Joe came in from cutting roses in his rose garden. He kissed Eva on the cheek and held out a lovely red rose.

"For you, my love. You are the best wife a preacher could ask for."

Then, he took the rose and put it between his teeth. He picked Eva up and swung her around, laughing at her struggling to get down. Then, he put her in a chair and knelt in front of her, handing her the rose again.

"We are so blessed, Eva, so blessed. I saw Grace leaving just now, and it's hard to believe she is the same person. God has done wonders with her and with Tina. You were a big part of that, supporting her with your friendship. I really meant it when I said you are the best wife a preacher could ever have. You are truly a helpmate. You are part of the reason our congregation just continues to keep growing. We are getting some more chairs, by the way, did I tell you?" he said, with a smile.

"Chairs aren't the problem anymore, Joe. Where to put them is the biggest problem," Eva replied, stroking his hair.

"Well, we are tearing down a wall from one of the old classrooms that joins the auditorium. That will seat about fifty more," said Pastor Joe. "But, we need to continue to pray that God's will be done in our growth, too. I certainly don't want to get ahead of Him, but He continually leads people to the church. I know in my heart that He will provide," he said, patting her on the knee.

"How about me making us a sandwich before I go help knock down the walls?" he said, laughing.

"Better take the boys with you. They are really good at tearing things up," laughed Eva.

CHAPTER SIX

Anna Cantrell had been Pastor Joe's secretary since the church originally began. They had only twenty five members when they first started meeting in the community room, years before. She had watched the church grow to the point where they were able to move into the old high school auditorium, thanks to the generosity of the school. Anna was an extremely competent secretary, and a well loved friend of the DuPriest family.

Her husband, Gary, had died five years before. Gary Cantrell had been one of the most valued members of the local police department. He made friends with practically everyone he met.

One afternoon, while playing basketball with some of the youth group from the church, Gary had suffered a major heart attack. When the paramedics arrived, they did their best to resuscitate him. There was nothing they could do to save him.

They hadn't had any children, although they had tried for years. Finally, the doctors told Anna she couldn't have children. Anna felt sad that she didn't have Gary's child to raise. After he died, her job at the church became her whole life.

Pastor Joe and Eva became very close to Anna after Gary

died. They treated her like one of their family. Therefore, when Pastor Joe noticed Anna becoming agitated one morning while looking out the window, he felt compelled to ask her what was wrong.

"It's that man, Pastor Joe. The one sitting in the green car that is parked out by the lake," she answered.

"What about him?" asked Pastor Joe, as he looked out the window and saw the green car parked outside the church.

"Well, it started about a month ago. I was at the grocery store late one night. It was after church one Wednesday night. I believe it was about nine-thirty. Anyway, I was walking to the parking lot from the store. All the clerks were gone that usually help people out with their groceries. I had my arms full, and when I tried to reach the keys in my purse, I dropped one of the bags there in the parking lot."

"This man came out of nowhere and picked up the bag. He was really friendly, and I thanked him for his help. They were starting to turn the lights out inside the store, so I hurried and got in my car and left."

"The next week, I took the church deposit to the bank. When I started back to my car, there was this same man getting in his car next to mine."

"I thought at the time it was a coincidence. He came over and opened my car door for me. He introduced himself as Albert Bankston. He said he remembered me from the grocery store."

"It seemed innocent enough that he would be at the bank. I told him my name, and that I worked at the church, and had to get back," said Anna.

"Then, two days later, it was on a Sunday morning, and as I came back from praying at the altar, I looked up and there he was, sitting about three rows behind where I had been sitting."

"He nodded at me, and I nodded back. When church was over, I went by my office to get some work to take home with me, and when I came out of the office, there he was in the hallway."

"It was dark, but I could tell it was him, Pastor Joe. He saw me looking at him, but he didn't say anything, he just stood there," she said.

"What in the world was he doing back there, Anna?" asked Pastor Joe.

"That's what I was wondering," said Anna. "And it really made me nervous, because I thought I was the only one in the building."

"Then, I looked up and saw Brother Eugene and Brother Earnest going in to put the offering in the safe. The man saw them and turned around and hurried away without saying anything."

"I have been getting some hang-up telephone calls, both at home and here at the church," she said. "It makes me wonder, you know."

"It makes me wonder, too, Anna" said Pastor Joe. "There are all kinds of people in this world. You need to be careful, living alone like you do."

"That is what I have been thinking," said Anna. "The other night, I heard my neighbor's dog barking outside, so I got out of bed and looked out the window. I saw this green car parked down the street about three houses down. It doesn't belong to anyone in the neighborhood. That's the same car that is parked outside now."

"Well, I am going to call Geoffrey Martin down at the police headquarters and ask him to run by here," said Pastor Joe.

Geoffrey had been Gary's partner on the force. He and his wife, Hope, were very dear friends of Anna's. They were members of the church, so Pastor Joe knew them well. Geoffrey had recently been promoted to Captain. Geoffrey would know what to do.

Pastor Joe reached for the phone. He walked over to

The Power House

look out of the window, just as the car pulled away. It was too far away for him to see the license plate.

He called the police station, anyway, and told Geoffrey what Anna had just shared with him about the man in the green car.

"Yeah, the man told her his name is Albert Bankston," said Pastor Joe. "It just seems strange that he would be following her to the bank, to church, and to her house, and now, here in the parking lot. Is there any way that you can check this guy out?"

"All we can do is drive by Anna's house at night and keep an eye on what's going on in her neighborhood. If we see the car there, we will check it out. If you see the guy at the church again, call me, and I will run by there," said Geoffrey.

"Thank you, Geoffrey," said Pastor Joe. "I will tell Anna. That should make her feel somewhat better about the situation, knowing you will be keeping an eye on her house in the evenings," he said, looking at Anna.

Anna listened to what Pastor Joe was saying to the policeman. She nodded her head, *yes*, indicating she would feel better knowing the police were patrolling her neighborhood.

A week passed, and Anna had neither seen nor heard from Albert Bankston. On Thursday morning, a floral delivery was made to the church. The delivery driver brought a large vase of twenty red roses and put it on Anna's desk, as she sat typing a letter for Pastor Joe. She turned, seeing the delivery driver, and the roses.

"Oh, Sam, those roses are gorgeous. Who's the lucky person?" she asked.

"I don't know, Mrs. Cantrell. There's a card with them. All I do is deliver. Gotta run. Lots of deliveries today," he said, as he hurriedly left her office.

Anna looked at the card, expecting to see the name of one of the younger staff members. She was surprised to see her own name on the card.

She opened the card, smiling, thinking Pastor Joe and Eva had sent her flowers. Her birthday was in two days.

"Maybe they got the date mixed up, and thought it was today," she thought.

She looked at the signature before she read the note. It was the initials *A.B.*

Frowning, she tried to think who *A.B.* might be. The realization that it might be Albert Bankston sent cold shivers down her spine. She read the note.

It said, "You sure look good in purple."

Anna gasped, then, made a beeline to Pastor Joe's office, where she found him sitting at his desk.

He looked up as Anna rushed into the room. She didn't say anything, just handed him the card. He looked at it, realizing from her anxious expression that something was bothering her about the card.

"It came with twenty red roses, Pastor Joe. I don't understand the meaning of the card, but I just *know* that it came from Albert Bankston."

"Take a deep breath, Anna. Now calm down and let's think this through."

He looked at the card again, scratching his chin as he considered what meaning the card had for Anna.

"When do you remember last wearing purple, Anna?"

"I don't have much purple in my wardrobe, Pastor Joe. Mostly I wear it in the fall or winter."

Suddenly, Anna's expression changed.

"The only purple I wear all the time is my robe," Anna gasped.

She looked at Pastor Joe and then leaned against the desk for support. Her knees had gotten weak at the thoughts she was having.

"Albert Bankston must have been looking through my windows at night," Anna thought.

Then, she remembered going outside the evening before

to call Sugar, her cat, to come into the house. *"Maybe Albert Bankston saw me then."*

Pastor Joe realized that Anna was having frightening thoughts. He noticed that she was turning very pale, and beginning to shake all over.

He got up from his chair and went to stand by her.

"Anna, I can only imagine what you must be thinking. But, I can see where you might possibly be right. Albert Bankston may be spying on you. Or, at least, he has to have been in the neighborhood. The reason I say that is pretty clear. You saw his car in the neighborhood, and now he sends the roses with the card saying you look good in purple."

Putting his hands on Anna's shoulders, he turned her to face him.

"Anna, please remember this. *"For God has not given us a spirit of fear, but of power, and of love, and of a sound mind,"* he quoted. "You need to keep a level head about this, Anna. If you start to panic, then he will be doing you damage without even coming near you."

"You are right, Pastor Joe. I know you are right," said Anna, standing straighter. She took a deep breath. "There has to be a way of dealing with this and I am going to find it."

"Eva and I are right here for you, Anna. You are welcome to come and stay with us for awhile, until we can determine exactly what is going on. In fact, I would like to *insist* that you stay with us, beginning tonight. But, I don't like that word *insist*. It's up to you, but I would feel better knowing you are with us than at your house alone, with someone possibly looking in your windows. Right now, I am going to go call Geoffrey again."

In less than half an hour, Captain Geoffrey Martin stood in Pastor Joe's study. Brett Young, one of the officers on the force, was with him. Brett had a notebook in his hand, and was making notes.

The captain had been in police work long enough to

know to take things like this seriously. So far, there had been no threats, but he recognized the beginning of a sequence suggesting that Anna was being stalked.

"Let me see the card, Anna," Geoffrey said.

He took the card from her, looked at the name of the florist, and wrote the name in the notebook.

"First thing we will do is go over to the florist and find out more about the man who sent the flowers. If he used a credit card, we will be able to trace his address. I would like to talk to this Mr. Bankston, if that is really his name," Geoffrey said.

"Oh, and by the way, Anna, I think it would be a good idea for you to take Pastor Joe and Mrs. DuPriest up on their offer to stay with them for a short time. At least, until we get to the bottom of this."

"Thanks, Geoffrey. I think it's a good idea, too, and I have already decided to do just that," replied Anna.

Eva took their older son, Paul, with her to meet Anna at her house to get her things together to stay with the DuPriest's. Paul carried her overnight bag and Eva took Anna's suit bag. They put them in Anna's car while she chased Sugar, her cat, across the yard. Finally, she caught him, and put him in her car. Then, she followed Eva and Paul back to their house.

Anna insisted on helping with dinner. She spent the following hour in the kitchen, making Pastor Joe's favorite Italian Cream cake for dessert. Eva prepared dinner while Anna made the cake. The two of them talked and laughed, enjoying one another's company. It helped take Anna's mind off the reason she was there that evening.

The next morning, when Anna arrived early to open the church, there was a canvas bag by the door. That was not unusual in itself, as Pastor Joe received many publications. The mailman or delivery drivers often left a canvas bag by the door if there was nobody to receive it.

The Power House

Anna stooped down to pick up the canvas bag. It was very heavy. She carried it inside the foyer, then untied the string and opened the bag.

Anna screamed when she saw the contents of the bag. At first, she thought it was Sugar, her cat. Then, she realized it was a toy stuffed animal cat that looked exactly like Sugar.

Someone had tied a brick around the stuffed cat's neck with a light piece of rope. There was something red and sticky inside the bag.

Anna didn't wait to investigate further.

She locked the foyer door that she had just entered, then, looked out the side panel window of the door.

There, parked half a block away, sat Albert Bankston in his green car. He could see her peering out the window and he knew she could see him sitting there. He sped away, accelerating in front of the church, leaving tire marks on the pavement.

Anna ran into her office and called Geoffrey Martin at the police station. She told him about the canvas bag, and about seeing Albert Bankston outside the church. She was now thoroughly terrified.

"I'll be right there, Anna. Keep all the doors locked. Nobody gets in. Do you understand? Unless it's Pastor Joe or someone you know. Otherwise, no one. Got it?" Geoffrey said, emphatically.

"I understand," said Anna. "But, Geoffrey, please hurry. I am really rattled."

Geoffrey instructed the dispatcher to call Pastor Joe and have him meet him and Brett at the church. Then, they got in the police car and started to the church. Pastor Joe was running up to the front door of the church when Geoffrey and Brett arrived. He was out of breath. Anna had already called him to tell him what she had found when she arrived at the church fifteen minutes earlier. He was concerned for her safety, at this point.

Geoffrey looked inside the canvas bag in the foyer. He reached down and ran his finger through the red, sticky liquid. Then he held it to his nose, smelling of it.

"Ketchup," he said. "It's ketchup, Anna."

Brett noticed something in the bag that Anna and Geoffrey had not seen earlier.

"Say, what's this?" Brett asked.

Brett took out his handkerchief and picked up a card that was tied to the stuffed animal's throat. Gingerly, he opened the card.

"Sugar sure looks good in red," the card read.

Anna looked at Pastor Joe. It was just like the card she had received with the flowers that read, "You sure look good in purple."

Anna didn't have to say a word. Pastor Joe, as well as the policemen, could tell how frightened she was.

"It's uncanny how much this stuffed toy looks like Sugar, isn't it?" Geoffrey said.

"I thought it *was* Sugar, when I first saw it. Then I remembered that he was at Pastor Joe's with me this morning," said Anna.

She started shaking, and began to cry. Pastor Joe moved to her side and placed an arm around her shoulder.

"This is enough for today, Anna," he said. "I am taking you back to spend the day with Eva."

"No, Pastor Joe, that's okay. I will be alright. Just give me a few minutes to compose myself. There is too much for me to get done today to go back home. I can't afford to wimp out on you. Besides, I am praying not to be fearful. I really don't want to give that man any power over me. But, I just don't understand what this is all about. Why is he doing this to me?"

Geoffrey Martin did not understand it, either. But, he was taking this as a serious threat now. He advised Pastor Joe to call a security office and have some security guards patrol the church grounds. He suggested he have one at his house, too, since Anna was staying there.

Pastor Joe agreed. It was obvious the man was a very disturbed individual to do something like this. Pastor Joe couldn't imagine why, either. Anna was one of the sweetest people he had ever known.

"Who would want to harm someone like Anna?" he asked Geoffrey.

Captain Geoffrey Martin was taking this situation with Anna very personal. Anna was a dear friend of his and his wife, Hope. She was the widow of his old partner, who had also been his best friend.

He wondered the same thing as Pastor Joe. He couldn't imagine who would want to harm Anna. But, he was dead set on finding out who was responsible for leaving the canvas bag at the church door, and sending the flowers.

"Good morning, Officers," said the lady behind the counter at the florist

"What brings you in so early this lovely day?" she asked with a cheerful smile.

"Police business, Ma'am," Geoffrey said, noticing the smile disappear from the woman's face.

"Oh. Well then, how may I help you?" she asked.

He showed her the card that Anna had received with the flowers, the card with the initials *A.B.* as the signature.

"Do you remember this man?" he asked her. "The one who sent these flowers?"

She hesitated for a moment, studying the card carefully.

"Why, yes I do. He was very strange, I remember now. He was insistent that I make certain there were *exactly* twenty red roses in that vase we were sending over to the church. Not twenty-one, mind you, or twenty-two, but, twenty exactly. He stayed until we finished them, then he counted them himself. I thought at the time it was very strange."

"Did he pay with a credit card?" asked Geoffrey.

The Power House

"No, sir, he didn't pay with a credit card. He paid with cash. He laughed, in fact, as he counted out twenty, one dollar bills. Of course, he had to come up with the tax, after that. I wondered at the time what it was with all the twenty stuff."

"Okay, Ma'am. Here's my card. If he should come back in here, don't act like anything is wrong, okay? Just go to the back of the store and call me immediately. If I am not at the station, have them radio me," said Geoffrey.

"Well, sure. I'll do that. What's going on, Officer?" she asked.

"Like I said, police business, Ma'am. That's all I am at liberty to say right now. Just call me if he comes back in, okay?" he said.

"I will. Of course I will," said the woman, running her hand over her hair, looking flustered.

Geoffrey Martin felt like he had the air let out of him. He was hoping and praying that the man had bought the flowers with a credit card. He would have been well on his trail, if he had. Finding Albert Bankston wasn't going to be as easy as Geoffrey had hoped.

Geoffrey and Brett went back by the church and told Anna that he had not been able to get a credit card to locate the man. At that moment, Pastor Joe came into Anna's office.

"Geoffrey, I know you are on duty right now. But, I would like to ask you to pray with Anna and me that something breaks in this situation that will let you find this guy. None of us will rest until he is located," said Pastor Joe.

"Pastor, I have been praying all morning for God to give Anna grace to deal with what she is going through. But, yes, by all mean's, let's pray," said Geoffrey. "Brett, would you like to join us in this prayer?"

"Uh, well, sure," said Brett, seeming to be a bit uncomfortable in the situation.

Pastor Joe, Anna, Geoffrey and Brett all joined hands and prayed that God would guide them to someone that

The Power House

could help reveal the whereabouts of Albert Bankston.

When Geoffrey went home that evening, he was talking to his wife, Hope, about what happened to Anna. Their daughter, Nicole, came into the room and stood behind the sofa, unnoticed. She overheard her father telling her mother about what happened at the church that day. He told her about finding the stuffed animal that looked exactly like Anna's cat, Sugar, in the canvas bag. Just before mentioning about the rope and the ketchup, he heard his daughter speaking to him.

"I saw a cat like that last week, Daddy," she said. "It is the only one I have ever seen that looked just like Aunt Anna's cat."

Geoffrey turned, quickly, to see his five year old daughter standing behind the sofa. He felt bad that she had heard the conversation. He was glad he had not yet told Hope about the ketchup part. But, he was very interested in what his daughter had just told him.

"Where, Nicky?" he asked. "Where did you see the cat?"

"I was with my friend Robin and her mother. She took us shopping with her. She said she had to go buy some get-well cards for her sister that was in the hospital. She left Robin and me in the toy section of the store to look at the stuffed animals. That is where I saw the cat like Sugar," she said.

"What store, honey, is what I want to know," he said gently.

"The Yellow Daisy, Daddy. You know I love that store. I found a big stuffed goldfish I want. I would name him Tuna," she giggled.

"Daddy, is Aunt Anna alright? I heard you saying some man was bothering her," she added, with concern in her young voice.

"She's fine, sweetie," Geoffrey said. "Don't worry about Aunt Anna. We will find that man and Aunt Anna is going to be fine."

The story had obviously bothered his daughter. That night, she came into the bedroom and asked if she could sleep with him and her mother. She hadn't done that in years. They pulled her under the covers with them. She slept soundly throughout the night.

Geoffrey didn't sleep well, though. He couldn't wait until morning to go to The Yellow Daisy. He wanted to ask some questions about a stuffed animal that looked like Sugar.

The first thing the next morning, he and Brett went by The Yellow Daisy. Geoffrey knew Anna's cat, Sugar, and he knew that he would be able to tell if the store had a stuffed animal like the one with the concrete block around its neck left in the canvas bag.

They entered the store, then, went to the back where Geoffrey had been many times with his daughter, Nicole. There, on the bottom shelf, were two more stuffed cats just like the one left at the church.

"Hi, Barbara," he said to the store manager. "How are you this morning?"

"Hi, Captain Martin," she said. "I am doing super duper. How about you?"

"I'm fine, Barbara. I need to know something. This is official business, okay?"

"Sure, Captain Martin. How can I help you?" she asked.

"Have you sold any of these lately?" he asked, holding up the cat.

"Well, as a matter of fact, yes I have. A guy came by the other day and was almost *gleeful* when he saw this cat. I asked him why, and he said that he couldn't believe he was lucky enough to find one exactly like he was looking for."

"Do you know if any of the other stores in town carry this same stuffed animal?" he asked.

"I know for certain they don't," Barbara said. "We have an exclusive on this company's products for a sixty mile radius in their marketing territory. They are more expensive than most of the stuffed animals. Kind of a specialty item."

"Do you remember if the man paid for the cat with a credit card or if he paid with cash?" asked Geoffrey.

He held his breath, waiting for Barbara to answer.

"Hmmm, let me see. Oh, I remember now. It was a credit card. I remember because Jodie was on the phone in the back and we had a hard time getting it to go through. That dial tone thing, you know."

Geoffrey couldn't believe what he was hearing. He was finally getting a break.

"Could you run back and find a copy of that card, please? It is very important."

"I went through them last evening. They are right here in the bag," said Barbara.

She pulled a bag from underneath the counter. She leafed through the credit card receipts, then, found the one she was seeking.

"Here it is, Captain Martin. Anthony Brandon. I remember, now."

"Anthony Brandon? Well, now, this is beginning to make some sense," he said, knowing he had heard the name somewhere before.

"Can I keep this for a day or two?"

"Well, I guess it will be okay, since it is police business. Sure, go ahead, Captain Martin, if it will help somebody," said Barbara.

"I can assure you that it will," said Geoffrey. "Oh, and Barbara, ring up this stuffed fish for me, okay? It's for Nicky. She's going to name him Tuna."

Geoffrey had Brett run a search on the credit card when they got back to the office. The card belonged to Anthony Brandon, a convicted felon who had committed aggravated armed robbery of a convenience store right in the same town. The arresting officer had been Gary Cantrell. Anthony Brandon was serving twenty years for aggravated armed robbery, and assault with a deadly weapon. Anthony had shot the convenience store clerk, hitting him in the ankle, as he was fleeing the scene of the crime.

"*Twenty years, twenty roses, twenty dollar bills,*" thought Geoffrey.

He was beginning to understand why Anthony Brandon might be terrorizing Anna. Gary was no longer around for Anthony to seek revenge from, so he was going after Anna.

"How did this guy get out, though?" he said to Brett.

He was scheduled to serve twenty years. There was no way he could have gotten paroled.

Geoffrey had Brett find the information he needed. In half an hour, the sergeant came into his office, with the scoop on Anthony.

After they were arrested and tried, Frank Livingston, the man who helped Anthony rob the convenience store, was sent to the same penal institution.

Frank was wanted in another state for murdering a bank teller, in a foiled bank robbery. He had bragged to Anthony about killing the bank teller during the robbery attempt, proudly giving him specific details of the crime.

Anthony realized he could use the information Frank had given him to help himself. He had turned state's evidence on him. In return, Anthony only served five years, and then was released.

He must have come back to town, looking for Gary Cantrell, only to find that Gary had died. For some reason, Geoffrey believed, Anthony wanted to seek revenge by terrorizing Anna. He hoped that is all he wanted to do.

With men like Anthony Brandon, you never could tell. He knew he had to find him.

That night, Anna went home. She turned the lights on in the house, and wore her purple robe from room to room.

Geoffrey Martin and four other policemen waited in the dark outside Anna's house. They were certain Anthony

Brandon had been watching the church when Anna left. One of the officers had tailed his green car from the church to his rented apartment on the other side of town. Brett had requested to remain inside the house, out of sight, to keep an eye on Anna.

Anna waited until eleven o'clock to turn out the lights and go to her bedroom. She went to her bed, and knelt in prayer.

Brett could see her from where he was crouched behind the sofa in the den.

"*She looks like an angel, there on her knees in the moonlight,*" he thought.

Brett had met Anna a few months earlier when he and Captain Martin were having lunch. Anna and Eva DuPriest had come in for coffee, and Captain Martin introduced everyone.

Brett thought Anna was a lovely lady, and would have liked to ask her out. But, then, Captain Martin had begun talking about her working as a secretary where he went to church. He told Brett about Gary, her husband, dying of a heart attack, and how well Anna had been able to carry on because of her strong faith in God.

Brett believed in God, but he had never gone to church very much after he grew up. He decided not to pursue asking her for a date, although he had found himself very attracted to her. He thought she wouldn't be interested in someone who didn't share her depth of faith.

But, tonight, the strong feeling to protect her was something he couldn't deny. She looked so vulnerable, there kneeling by the bed.

Anna finished her prayers, and glanced at the doorway. She realized Brett had been watching her from where he was hiding, and she smiled at him.

She said, "I said one for you, too, Brett. I asked God to bless you and watch over all of you. And, Brett, thank you."

Then she closed the door and went to sit on her bed and wait.

All at once, the policemen outside the house heard a car stop down the block. They saw the lights go off on the car, and heard a car door being closed quietly, intentionally not slammed. Geoffrey said something softly into his radio, warning everyone to keep quiet.

Still, they waited. They couldn't hear anything for a few minutes. Then, they heard the patio door being smashed, and the sound of glass shattering.

Geoffrey ran to the back of the house, just as Anthony Brandon stepped into the house through the broken patio door.

Suddenly, the lights in the house came on. Not expecting anyone other than Anna to be there, Anthony was startled, and it took a few moments for him to realize what was happening.

Brett came from behind the sofa, gun pointed directly at Anthony Brandon.

"Drop it, Brandon," he said.

Anthony had a gun in his hand, and had used the butt of the gun to break the glass door on the patio. He was so startled by Brett's being in the house that he immediately dropped the gun on the floor. Brett shoved the gun out of the way with his foot. Geoffrey and the other officers came into the house.

Anthony Brandon was going back to jail for a long time.

Pastor Joe was waiting at home, praying, with Eva, for the safety of Anna and the police team. They knew what the plan was, and they knew it involved a potentially dangerous situation for Anna, and the officers, as well. The telephone rang, and Pastor Joe jumped up from where he and Eva had been praying. He ran to answer the phone.

"They got him, Pastor Joe. Thank God, it's over," said Anna. "He broke the patio door and came in with a gun. He

The Power House

intended to harm me, that is for sure. Geoffrey and some of the other officers just took him out to the police car. I didn't even come out of the bedroom until I knew he was gone."

"Praise God! Oh, Anna, I am so happy to hear that they got him."

"They got him, Eva," he said to his wife, who was anxiously awaiting news.

"Like I told you the other day, Anna, we just don't know what he was capable of," said Pastor Joe. "You know as well as I do that there are two forces working in this world. He certainly was working on the dark side, wasn't he? But, thank God you are alright. Anna, do you want to come back over and stay here with Eva and me tonight?"

"No, Pastor Joe. But, thanks for being so thoughtful. I will be fine now," she said. "God is so good. It was just a miracle that Nicky walked in and heard Geoffrey talking about that stuffed cat she saw that looked like Sugar. If she hadn't, I don't know if they would have caught the man before he did me harm."

After she hung up the phone, Anna and Geoffrey held hands once more and thanked God for helping them through the situation. Brett stood and bowed his head while they prayed.

They had asked for God for His help in finding Albert Bankston , and they were faithful to give Him the glory for it when it came.

CHAPTER SEVEN

Brett's attention to Anna had not gone unnoticed by Geoffrey, even through all the turmoil of trying to find Albert Bankston, *a.k.a.*, Anthony Brandon.

Geoffrey was talking with Hope early that morning, telling her about how everything had turned out. He finished the part about arresting Anthony, and how he would be facing a stiff jail sentence. Then, he mentioned how Brett had seemed very attentive to Anna.

Like most women, Hope loved the possibility of a romance. She had worried about Anna for years, ever since Gary had died.

Anna was a beautiful young woman, and Hope and Geoffrey had always hoped that Anna would find someone else someday. As far as they were concerned, she was much too young to spend the rest of her life alone.

Each time Hope mentioned the idea of Anna finding someone else, Anna told her she still was in love with Gary and it wouldn't be fair to someone else to start a relationship. She never planned to marry again. Hope had stopped pushing the idea several years back.

"Timing is everything, Geoffrey. Maybe by now she is ready to meet someone," she said excitedly. Hope really liked Brett.

"He is perfect for Anna," she said. "He is fun-loving, intelligent, and not bad to look at, either, if you don't mind my saying so," she added, with an impish smile

"Oh, he is, is he?" said Geoffrey, smashing a throw pillow playfully in Hope's face.

They laughed for a few moments, then, Geoffrey said, "You know, I usually steer away from these kinds of things. You know what I mean, fixing people up and all. But, this time you might have a good idea. I agree with you, those two would be great together."

"Then, let's invite them both to dinner this Saturday," said Hope, excitedly. "I will tell Anna that we are inviting Brett, and you tell him we are inviting Anna. That way, we are above board with everyone, and they will have their choice of saying yes or no."

"Great idea. I will ask Brett tomorrow. You call Anna," he said.

"Done deal," said Hope.

At first, Anna tried to explain to Hope all the reasons she couldn't come to dinner at their house. They were all the same reasons Hope had heard from Anna before about her not meeting someone. This time, Hope was ready to address each issue Anna mentioned. Soon, Anna ran out of reasons and agreed to go.

Brett, on the other hand, jumped at the invitation. He had decided that he would like to get to know Anna better. There was something about that night when he saw her kneeling beside her bed, praying. He would never forget the way she looked, so lovely, so serene when she was talking with God.

God. Now, there is where I may fall short when it comes to Anna, he thought.

Saturday night, Brett and Anna were sitting at the dinner table at Geoffrey and Hope Martin's house. Hope had made gumbo, a Caesar salad, and garlic bread. She had brownies and hot fudge sauce for dessert. Nicky had hot fudge sauce smeared all over her face, after she finished her dessert.

"Go on upstairs and wash your face, Nicky," said Hope. "You look like you fell in a mud puddle," she laughed.

"Mommy, can I stay up in my room and watch my new video Aunt Anna brought me?"

"Absolutely, Sweetie. You go right ahead. Then, when the video is over, get your pj's on and get ready for bed, okay?" said her mother.

"Goodnight everybody. You won't see me again, because I always get sleepy watching videos," Nicky said.

Anna got up from the table and bent down to hug Nicky.

"God bless you, sweet girl," she said, as she rocked Nicky back and forth. "You know, you helped your Daddy solve that case. I will always be grateful to you for that."

"I got a reward, "said Nicky, holding up her stuffed fish named Tuna. "Does that mean I am an honorary detective?" she asked, with a big grin.

"Absolutely, honey," said Geoffrey, laughing along with the rest of them.

Nicky made her rounds of the table, giving hugs to everyone. She had Brett lean down so she could whisper something in his ear. The others could hear her stage whisper.

"Aunt Anna is really pretty, isn't she?"

He smiled and mussed her hair.

"You bet, honey. You bet," he said.

Everyone waited until Nicky left the room to burst out laughing.

After dinner, the grownups went into the living room to visit. They talked briefly about what had happened with Anthony Brandon, then, Hope said it was time to change the subject and have some fun. She brought out a deck of cards, and they all played canasta until late in the evening. Everyone had a wonderful time, and shared many laughs.

Brett asked if he could drive Anna home. Hope and Nicky had gone by to pick her up. Hope knew *someone* would have to take Anna home.

"That would be lovely," she answered. "Let me get my sweater."

She went into the den to get the sweater she had left on the back of the sofa when she had arrived. Hope followed her into the room.

"Well?" she asked. "What do you think?"

"About Brett? He is a very nice man. I like him. Hope, I really enjoyed this evening. It took my mind off all that has happened, and that was something that was difficult to do. But, somehow being here with all of you this evening was like old times when Gary was living," she said.

Anna hung her head.

"I still miss him very much, Hope. But, you know, I am glad I came tonight. I am surprised at how much I enjoyed Brett's company."

Hope told Geoffrey, word for word, what Anna had said, after they left. They hugged one another. That night, when they got in bed, Geoffrey reached for Hope's hand in the dark.

"Hope, honey, let's pray that, if this is God's will, Anna and Brett will fall in love and get married. That should be our prayer, don't you think?"

"Geoffrey, that is so sweet. I agree. Let's pray that prayer together," said Hope.

And, together they prayed for God's will to be done in Anna and Brett's lives, and in theirs, as well.

Brett had gone out with quite a few women in his younger years, however, he had never found one with whom he wanted to share the rest of his life.

He was in love with Anna before they reached her driveway.

He loved everything about her. The way she dressed, the way she carried herself. The way she spoke, the way she looked directly into his eyes when he was talking to her.

He thought she was beautiful and gentle. Such a contradiction to most of the women he had dated.

Anna was very attracted to Brett, as well.

When he asked her to go to dinner with him the next evening, she knew in her heart there were questions that needed answering before continuing the relationship.

Brett was making no guesswork out of the way he felt about her. Things were moving too fast for Anna, not knowing all she felt she should know about Brett.

She invited Brett to come in for coffee. He was not surprised when the conversation turned to religion.

"I don't have a regular church," he answered to Anna's question about where he attended church. "I go on occasion. Not regularly. Captain Martin has been trying to get me to go with his family to your church. I think I might do that now," he added, with a smile.

"Are you a Christian?" asked Anna.

This was a big question in her mind, as to where the relationship might be going.

"I was baptized when I was thirteen, because some of my friends were. I quit going to church regularly when I got out of high school and went to college. I believe in God, if that's what you are asking."

"There is just so much to praise and thank Him for," said Anna. "I can't imagine not going to worship the Lord every Sunday morning; after all He has done for me. I truly love the Lord, as it says in Mark, *with all my heart and with all my soul and with all my strength.*" To me, it's like I once heard someone say, "The heart of the matter is really the matter of the heart. And, Brett, I truly have a heart for God."

"I understand, Anna," said Brett. "I would like to know the Lord like you and Hope and Captain Martin do. I could see the faith you had, even in the face of the adversity of being stalked by that guy. It was inspiring, truly inspiring.

Who *wouldn't* want that for themselves? I have been thinking about that ever since the other night, when I saw you in your bedroom, on your knees in prayer."

"Then, since you have asked me for dinner tomorrow night, let me ask you to come to church with me on Sunday morning," she said. "That's fair, isn't it?"

"I would be glad to go to church with you, Anna," said Brett. "I know we just met, but I would like to tell you that I think you are very special. I promise to treat you that way, too. You are such a beautiful, sweet lady."

"Thank you, Brett," said Anna. "I can tell already how nice a guy you are. And, of course, Hope and Geoffrey have expounded on that topic a great deal, too, not to mention little Nicky. She is already trying to pair us up," she laughed.

The next morning, Eva came by the church to bring some fresh pastries to Pastor Joe and the staff. Anna told Eva and Pastor Joe about her dinner with Brett, at the Martin's the night before.

"And, you are going out with him again tonight!" exclaimed Pastor Joe.

He took Eva by the hands and danced her around the room, laughing, while singing, "*This could be the start of something big.*"

Eva laughingly said, "Joe, you stop that. You are embarrassing Anna."

Anna laughed and said, "That's okay, Eva. I am used to his shenanigans."

Brett went to church with Anna that Sunday. They continued to see one another for three months, with Brett going to church with Anna each Sunday morning.

One particular Sunday morning, Anna noticed that Brett's demeanor had changed drastically from the first time he attended with her, months earlier. He sat listening intently to the sermon. He was very interested in what was being taught.

The Power House

Today Pastor Joe was speaking on the holiness of God. He quoted from Ephesians, *"we should be holy and without blame before Him."*

Brett had been studying his Bible each evening before he went to bed. He wanted that walk with the Lord that Anna had. He wanted to know Him intimately, as Geoffrey and Hope did.

Pastor Joe began the altar call. Brett found himself concentrating on the holiness of God. All at once, he realized that he wanted to stand before God as holy and without blame. He felt the need for the clean and pure heart that Pastor Joe so often talked about. Brett was amazed at the depth of his feelings about the Lord, at that moment.

God, Creator of all things, he thought. *Jesus, Incarnate, dying for me.*

Brett looked at Anna, who was praying beside him in the pew.

He took her hand and asked, "Will you come down front and pray with me?"

Anna shook her head, and together they went to the altar. There, kneeling at the altar with Anna, Brett received Jesus as his personal Savior.

Geoffrey, Hope and Nicky came down to stand with them, after he had made his decision for Christ. It was something he had done as a child, because his friends were doing it, but his heart was bursting to make a real public profession of faith now, as a man.

Anna cried tears of joy and rejoiced in her heart over Brett's decision. What a joyous day it was for Anna and the Martin family that Brett had made a choice to walk with God.

Pastor Joe and Eva were also extremely happy that Brett had found the Lord. They could tell that Anna was very serious about Brett, but they also knew the relationship would never have a chance progress as far as Anna was concerned, unless he was a Christian.

A month later, on a beautiful Sunday afternoon, Brett and Anna were married in the sanctuary. The church was filled to capacity with well-wishers. Everyone loved Anna. She had been there from the very beginning, when the church met in the community room.

Anna had two matrons-of-honor. One was Eva, the other Hope. Geoffrey Martin was the best man. Nicky was the flower girl. Paul and Joey were ushers. It was a large wedding, a day filled with plenty of beautiful flowers and sunshine.

Brett looked handsome in his dress uniform. All the officers on the force who were not on duty attended, and in honor of Brett's wedding, they also wore their dress uniforms.

Anna sat in the bride's room, waiting for the music to begin. She was thinking that she would never have dreamed five and a half years before, after losing Gary, that she could ever be this happy again.

She would never forget Gary and the wonderful love they had shared. But, she gave thanks to God for bringing Brett into her life, even in the way she met him.

If she had not gone through the experience with Anthony Brandon, she and Brett would never have gotten together. It was just another example of God turning evil to good.

"The music is starting," said Hope, peeking in the door at Anna.

Anna stood, adjusted her dress, and started down the aisle on the arm of her good friend, Geoffrey Martin, to marry the man she loved.

With each step she took, she said in her heart, "Thank you, Lord. Thank you, Lord."

CHAPTER EIGHT

Five months had passed since the wedding of Brett and Anna Young. Pastor Joe had never seen Anna so happy. He was pleased that Anna and Brett had found one another.

As he entered the church that morning, he was remembering the story of the Martin family and how they had asked God's will for the union on the night they had Brett and Anna to dinner the first time. Their prayers were answered, because it was obvious this was truly a union blessed by God.

I guess I am just an old sap for romance, he thought, smiling, and whistling, as he entered the building.

He came into Anna's office just as she was answering the telephone. All at once, her expression changed to one of total astonishment. She finished her conversation, then, carefully hung up the telephone, her hand shaking as she replaced the receiver. For a moment, she sat staring into space.

Pastor Joe walked over to her desk and said, anxiously, "Anna, are you alright?"

Anna came out of her trancelike state when she realized Pastor Joe was talking to her.

"Hmmm? Oh, yes, sir. I am just fine. Pastor Joe, would it be alright with you for me to take my lunch hour early today?" she asked.

"Of course, Anna, go right ahead. Susan is here. She can catch the phones."

Anna lost no time in getting her purse and going to her car. She left the parking lot in a great hurry. Ten minutes later, she was entering the front door of the police station.

"Excuse me, will you please page Brett Young?" she asked the clerk at the desk.

"Certainly," said the desk clerk. "I just saw him in the back at the copier."

In a few minutes, Brett Young came to the front of the building to greet his wife.

"Anna, honey, what's going on? You are white as a sheet."

He took her arm and led her to his office.

"Brett, I had a phone call a little while ago. It was from Dr. Stratton's office. Brett, he said that we are going to have a baby."

Brett stopped in his tracks and looked at Anna. He took her by the shoulders.

"What? A baby? Are they sure?" he asked. "Anna, I *pray* they are *right*. You know I love children. But, I thought you said you were told you couldn't have children."

"Dr. Stratton told me it must have been because of Gary, not because of me, after all. He said I am three months pregnant. Brett, we are going to have a child!"

"Hallelujah!" he said. "Anna, a baby. Our baby!"

He picked her up and swung her around, then stopped suddenly and put her down.

"Oh, no," he said. "I have got to be more careful with you from now on."

He looked anxious about having swung her around.

"Don't be silly," Anna laughed. "I'm not made of glass, just because I'm pregnant."

They were both ecstatic about having a child. Neither had ever expected such a blessing.

Anna told Pastor Joe the news as soon as she got back to the church. She had wanted to tell him earlier, but felt Brett should be the first to know. Pastor Joe was thrilled for Anna. It seemed God was continuing to bless her with good things.

"Anna, I can't think of anyone who would be a better mother than you," he said, with all sincerity.

"I can't believe it, Pastor Joe. But, you know, with God, all things *are* possible."

During the next four months, Anna was given a great amount of attention by her husband, Brett. He treated her like a china doll, certain she was going to break something if she moved the wrong way. She laughed at his concern over her, but thought it was extremely sweet, too.

As time for the birth drew near, there were many baby showers. The people in the church were wonderful to Brett and Anna.

One of the men was a carpenter, and he built a special cradle for the baby.

There were many hand knitted baby sweaters and caps, lovingly done by the ladies in the church.

Anna planned to work until three weeks before the due date for the birth of the baby. She planned to take off for a few weeks, then, bring the baby to work with her, so they could be together. Pastor Joe was all for the idea.

The ultrasound had shown that the baby was a little boy. Anna and Brett had chosen the name of David Joseph for their son.

One afternoon, a month before the baby was due, Anna began experiencing labor pains. She became alarmed at the suddenness of the pains, as well as their intensity. She quickly buzzed Pastor Joe on the intercom.

"Pastor Joe," she gasped. "Please come out here, and hurry!"

Pastor Joe dropped his pen, where he had been composing the Sunday sermon. He ran down the hallway to Anna's

The Power House

office. She was bending over in pain, sitting at her desk.

He took one look at her face and picked up the telephone and called for an ambulance. As he hung up the phone, Anna fainted, and Pastor Joe caught her as she began to fall.

Half an hour later, Brett Young entered the emergency room at the hospital, at a dead run.

He had been involved with working a traffic accident when he got the call from the station that his wife had been taken to the hospital in an ambulance.

Brett saw Eva and Pastor Joe sitting outside in the waiting room. They looked concerned. He went directly to them and asked about Anna and the baby.

"We don't know anything yet, Brett. They have had her in there for about ten minutes. Her doctor was making rounds at the hospital when we arrived, so he is with her now," said Eva.

"Brett, we just have to wait until the doctor comes out. But, since you are here now, let's pray."

They sat in the waiting room and prayed for the safety of Anna and the baby. Brett paced the floor, waiting for the doctor to come out and tell them something. He had waited for ten minutes, nervously pacing back and forth, when he saw Dr. James coming towards him. He sprinted down the hall to meet him.

"What's going on, Dr. James? How is Anna?" he asked.

"You need to come with me right away, Brett. I know you and Anna planned for you to be there when the baby was born. It's about to happen," he said.

"Now?" asked Brett. "Dr. James, the baby isn't due for another month," he said, frightened for Anna and their child.

"Well, babies have a mind of their own. He is ready to be born, and there is nothing we can do about it now. Come on, Brett, get into these scrubs and let's get on in there," he said, hurriedly.

Brett put on the green scrubs he was being given by the nurse, and adjusted the mask over his nose and mouth.

He said a silent prayer, then looked at the doctor and said, "I'm ready."

Anna was conscious when Brett came into the room. She looked at him and smiled, weakly.

"Brett, you look so worried. I can only see your forehead, but you have about five lines running across it from your frown. Don't worry, honey. The Lord did not give us this baby to take him away from us so soon. Little David will be just fine."

With those words, she began another contraction, and Brett stood aside as the doctor delivered their tiny baby boy.

David Joseph Young came into the world with a weak little cry. To Brett, it sounded like a kitten meowing. It was not the loud, healthy cry of a newborn baby that he had heard about from the mothers who had been discussing the birth of their children with Anna. Brett knew that much, although he had never before witnessed the birth of a baby.

The nurse took the baby from the doctor and carried him to a small table at the side of the room. She suctioned the baby's nose, and did all the things nurses do to newborns. Then, she turned to Brett and offered the baby to him. He took his son in his arms.

His first thought was, *he is way too small.*

He could barely feel the weight of the child in his arms. He had never seen anything so tiny in his life.

The baby weighed three pounds. Dr. James and the nurses were tending to Anna.

Anna asked to hold the baby. Brett took the baby to her, and laid him beside her. Anna looked at little David and began to cry. She looked at Brett, knowing that he was frightened for her and the baby. She put her lips against David's cheek and kissed him.

"I am not going to wait to dedicate our baby to the Lord

in church, Brett. I want you to hold my hand right now and put your other hand on our child. Pray, Brett. Pray with me now and, together, let us dedicate our baby to God."

"Yes, darling, I will. Let's pray," said Brett.

Brett took a deep breath, and wiped the tears from his face. He did not see Pastor Joe and Eva as the nurse led them into the room. When they saw that he was beginning to pray, they stopped where they were and bowed their heads.

"Well, Lord, here we are. The three of us. Anna, me, and little David Joseph. Mother, father and child. We are now parents, Lord. You gave us this tiny miracle. We dedicate him to you, Dear Lord, with all our hearts. We acknowledge you as the giver of life. We thank you for David Joseph, Lord. We ask that you strengthen him and bless him with health. He is so tiny, Lord, but we know that nothing is too difficult for You. Anna and I ask that, if it is your will, you would give us the opportunity to raise this child in health, and in a Christian home filled with love for you, and for our little baby boy."

Brett's voice broke, and he began to sob openly, looking down at the tiny, innocent baby cradled in Anna's arms.

Pastor Joe and Eva walked to the bedside and stood with Brett. Pastor Joe put his arm around Brett, comforting him.

Anna looked up at Eva and pulled the receiving blanket back, so that Eva could see David Joseph. Eva reached down and took his tiny hand in the crook of her finger. As she felt his tiny fingers close around her own, Eva felt her maternal instincts stronger than she had since Joey had been born. Tears slid down her face as she surveyed the mother and child. She prayed silently, with her eyes closed.

"We have to take him now," said the nurse. "We have to put him in an incubator."

Anna let the nurse take David from her arms. The doctor ordered a mild sedative for Anna, and about five minutes later, she drifted into a restless sleep. Brett stayed by her side, watching her toss and turn in her sleep.

Each day for the next two weeks, Anna and Brett stayed with their baby as often as they were allowed. Anna had been released from the hospital three days after David Joseph was born.

The members of the church started a vigil, with some of them coming to the church each night to pray together for baby David Joseph.

Pastor Joe and Eva visited with Brett and Anna as often as possible. They were all waiting for a miracle.

One afternoon, Dr. James had his nurse call Anna and Brett and ask them to come to the hospital. She would not tell them why, just that the doctor asked that they come.

When they arrived, he told them Baby David Joseph was gaining weight, and in Dr. James' words, had *turned the corner* in making progress towards survival. He wanted to keep him for a few more weeks, but he felt very good about the baby's prognosis.

Three weeks later, Brett and Anna took their tiny son home with them and placed him in the handmade cradle in their bedroom. There was a beautiful nursery down the hall from them, but there was no way they would put David in the nursery after all the time they had been away from him.

Brett and Anna looked down at their child. David seemingly smiled in his sleep, as babies often do.

"He's watching the angels dance," said Anna, with a smile. "That's what my grandmother used to say when babies smiled in their sleep."

A month later, Brett and Anna dedicated their child to the Lord, once again. This time, it was in the church, in front of the entire congregation.

Anna held baby David up so all the congregation could see him.

Smiling through her tears, she said, "How many of you out there know, without a doubt, that *with God, all things are possible?"*

The congregation stood to their feet, clapping their hands, thanking God for His goodness and His mercy, and for the life of David Joseph Young.

CHAPTER NINE

Pastor Joe woke earlier than usual the next morning, so he went to his study at the church. He arrived at seven a.m. He had some correspondence to catch up on, and he wanted to complete that before his first meeting for that day. Anna had told him on Friday afternoon that his eight a.m. appointment on Monday was with a young man who wanted to talk with Pastor Joe about performing his wedding.

The time went by so swiftly that he looked surprised when Anna tapped on his door and told him his eight o'clock appointment had arrived. Stacking the papers he was working on together, he sat them aside and told Anna to send the man in.

"Pastor Joe, good morning," said the young man, as he entered the study.

"Good morning, Matthew," said Pastor Joe, as he got up to shake his hand.

He was a little surprised when he realized who was there to see him. Matthew Johnson had been faithfully coming to church for the past few years. He loved the Lord and was always one of the first to walk to the altar to pray, or to worship on Sunday morning.

Pastor Joe had observed the countenance of the young

man on various occasions and found him to be reverent and humble in the house of the Lord. He was always smiling and talking with the other young adults when he attended functions outside the church.

A well-rounded young man, thought Pastor Joe.

He was happy to think of Matthew having found a future bride. It certainly seemed to Pastor Joe that Matthew would make a good husband for some young woman.

"It's good to see you, Matthew. Anna said you wanted to talk to me about getting married in a couple of weeks. Congratulations. Have I met the young lady?"

"Only in passing, Pastor Joe," said Matthew. "I brought her to church with me a couple of times, but we just shook hands with you when we were leaving the church. She lives in another town, but she will be moving here after the wedding. I wanted to ask if you will marry us. But knowing how deeply you feel about partners being *equally yoked*, as you call it, I wanted to tell you a story of what happened in church one Sunday. So *you* can be sure, like I am, that I am marrying someone who loves the Lord like I do."

"Well, Matthew, you are a little ahead of me here, because I was going to ask to meet with the two of you before the marriage. I still want to do that. But, I am also interested in hearing what you have to tell me. So, go ahead."

Matthew took a deep breath and said, "Pastor Joe, you know that I love the Lord."

Pastor Joe shook his head, acknowledging that he, indeed, knew of Matthew's devotion to the Lord.

"Well, here's the thing. Susan has gone to church most of her life. She has always loved the Lord, but she never seemed to want to go to the altar on Sundays to pray. She always seemed self-conscious about talking about her walk with the Lord. The more I talked about how I felt, the less she would open up with me about her feelings about certain things. Like scripture. Or about situations in life where people have to make decisions based on what the *world* would think about them, rather than what God would have them do. I made the mistake of saying that to her one night when we were talking about some people we both know."

He looked down, frowning, remembering that conversation with Susan.

Pastor Joe interrupted Matthew asking, "What exactly did you say to her?"

"Well, we were talking about an issue involving reading certain authors and how they all had a different take on what the Bible says."

"Susan just said, "Well, Matthew, everyone doesn't interpret things the same way. So, I suppose it is alright for them to think the way they want. Even if the Bible says something, it's okay if people decide not to take some of it literally."

Pastor Joe raised his eyebrows at that.

"Anyway, I made the mistake of saying to her, "Well, that is the way people in the *world* think, but not how Christians should think."

"I could see I had said the wrong thing when she started turning red. Pastor Joe, her face was red as a beet and she got up off the sofa and insisted that I take her home, right away. I tried to get her to open up and talk to me. And I tried to explain what I meant about what I had said, about the way people in the *world* think, but there was no getting through to her at that point."

"She said, very seriously, "Matthew, I want to go home, right now, and I have to tell you this. I am not sure I will ever come back here, much less marry you. You obviously feel you are superior and much more *holy* than my friends and I are."

"Uh-oh," said Pastor Joe. "This isn't sounding very good."

"Well, the story doesn't end there, thank God," said

Matthew. "The next day was Saturday, so I called and asked her if she would like to go out to dinner."

"She said right away, "No. I would *not* like to go to dinner or any other place with you, Matthew. I thought I made myself perfectly clear."

"So, I said, "Okay, I promise you this. I will leave you alone and stop asking you to go out if you will just say you will go to church with me on Sunday. Then I said, "Susan, we have had so many good times. Please don't let this one thing separate us forever. I love you, and I still want to marry you. Please just go to church with me just one more Sunday."

"She didn't say anything for a few minutes, then, she said, "Well, okay, I'll go. But, I don't want to discuss what we were discussing all over again, if that's what you are thinking."

"I told her it was a deal. So, I picked her up Sunday morning. She was in town staying with her aunt. All the way to church, she hardly said a word. When I stop the car, I usually go around and open the door for her," said Matthew.

"Of course," said Pastor Joe.

"Well, this time, the minute the car stopped, she jumped out and literally slammed the car door and starting stalking, not walking, up the sidewalk to the church. I had to run to keep up with her. She was still mad at me about the conversation we had, and was wishing she hadn't told me she would go to church with me that morning."

"When we got in church, she sat by me, but as far away as she could without touching me. I was really worried at that point. Not at her being mad at me, but worried that I had made a mistake in thinking she was right for me. It really had me going," said Matthew, swinging his foot back and forth, as he talked.

At this point, Pastor Joe, too, was wondering if maybe Matthew hadn't made a mistake. But, here was Matthew asking him to perform the ceremony, so something, undoubtedly, must have happened to make him change his mind. Pastor Joe was interested to hear what it was.

"That morning, the first song the choir sang was "Change My Heart O' God". I sat there listening to them sing and prayed, "Lord if there is something I need to change about *my* heart, please show it to me today, before it is too late."

"When you finished your sermon, I started praying about our situation and thinking about the conversation we had several nights before. I felt uncomfortable sitting there in the pew, so I got up went up to pray at the altar, like I sometimes do."

"When I knelt at the altar, I said, "Lord, if you want me to marry Susan - if this union is to take place - if it is your will, Lord, please soften her heart and have her come kneel beside me."

"Pastor Joe, the words barely left my lips before Susan was on her knees beside me with her hand in mine. All I could do was cry and hug her," said Matthew, with a slight catch in his voice.

Pastor Joe knew there was more to the story - that something had to have happened to change Susan's heart. He waited for Matthew to continue.

"Susan told me, after we left the service, that when I got up to go to the altar it actually made her even angrier, because she thought I was trying to be *holier than thou*, so to speak."

"Well, about that time, she said you were calling people to repentance, to come to Christ. But, also, you were speaking to people who were already Christians."

"She said you spoke on Paul's charge to Timothy about *fighting the good fight, finishing the race, and keeping the faith*. You exhorted Christians to continue to read their Bibles and listen to the word of God."

"I am sorry to have to say it, but I was praying so hard that I wasn't listening to what you read that morning, but Susan said you then read the passage from 2 Timothy about all scripture being the inspiration of God."

"Here," he said. "I have it right here. Let me read it to you, so I can show you what I mean when I tell you the rest of the story."

Matthew pulled a piece of paper from his shirt pocket.

"But you must continue in the things which you have learned and been assured of, knowing from whom you have learned them. And that from childhood you have known the Holy Scriptures, which are able to make you wise for salvation through faith which is in Jesus Christ. All Scripture is given by inspiration of God and profitable for doctrine, for reproof and for correction, for instruction in righteousness, that the man of God may be complete, thoroughly equipped for every good work."

"Susan told me she thought of the argument we had about the word of God. She said the Lord really convicted her about what she had said about some people maybe being right in not taking every word of the Bible as truth, but interpreting the Bible to suit themselves. She said those words, *"all Scripture is the inspiration of God"*, really got to her."

"Then she said that the Holy Spirit spoke to her heart and said, "Susan, it is not Matthew that is wrong. His heart is right. It is YOU, Susan.""

"She said that she acknowledged to the Lord that she knew in her heart she had been very wrong in saying what she had about the Word of God. She acknowledged that His word *is* Truth."

Pastor Joe moved to the edge of his seat, listening attentively to what Matthew was saying. He loved it when the Holy Spirit touched someone.

"She told me that at that moment her body was like it was on fire, from the top of her head, to the soles of her feet.

She said she bowed her head and said, "Lord, please forgive me. Thank you for Matthew. Please change my heart, purge me with your fire. I give for my life to you, and I *believe* your word as true and holy. I was so wrong to defend those people who believe otherwise."

"Now, here is the wonderful end to the story, Pastor Joe," said Matthew excitedly, rubbing his hands together, obviously delighted with what he was about to tell Pastor Joe.

"She told me that, no sooner had those words left her lips, than she found herself kneeling at the altar with her hand in mine. She doesn't have any recollection of how she got down there. Just that she looked up and was looking into the eyes of her new husband to be."

Matthew was laughing and crying at the same time, recalling those precious moments that changed the course of his and Susan's lives.

Pastor Joe slapped his hand on the desk in front of him.

"Praise the Lord Almighty!" cried Pastor Joe. "Thank you, Lord, for touching Susan's heart and showing her the truth about your Word."

"Amen," said Matthew.

"She's the one, Pastor Joe. God answered my prayer right there in the sanctuary. He gave me my answer. She's the one, and it's within His will. I want you to marry us in the sanctuary, where he put us together. Will you do it?"

"Yes, Matthew, I would be happy to marry the two of you. I am honored to marry a couple who chooses to walk with God."

"Of course, I still want to meet with the two of you together, but yes, I will marry you," he assured Matthew.

Matthew got up from his chair and came around the desk and hugged Pastor Joe.

"Thank you, Pastor Joe. I can't wait to tell Susan. We can meet with you whenever you want."

"We'll check with Anna on your way out, Matthew. She

knows my schedule better than I do. Now, come, let's pray for this union that God has ordained and thank Him for changing Susan's heart. What a mighty God we serve!" said Pastor Joe.

When they finished praying, Pastor Joe and Matthew went to Anna's office.

"Anna, three things. First, schedule an appointment for me to meet with Matthew and Susan, as soon as possible. Second, schedule a wedding. And third, order another chair. We will be gaining a new member, and she's got to have a place to sit!" Pastor Joe said, laughing and slapping Matthew on the back.

CHAPTER TEN

For many years, Pastor Joe's church had been known throughout the Christian community as a place where things got done. Plans were always in progress for new projects as soon as the current project was finished.

A new program called Community Power Outreach had been activated within the past month and was succeeding in bringing new people into the church to hear the word of God.

The wonderful thing was that the majority of the members were willing to give of their time and energy, as well as their resources, in doing something to further spread of the Gospel of Christ.

Because of the growth of the church, and the limitations of the building to contain those coming, Pastor Joe was having a meeting with a committee of elders that evening to talk about knocking out some more classroom walls, or the possibility of putting some mobile classrooms behind the church.

Pastor Joe had already introduced the ideas, and the final decisions were to be made at eight o'clock that evening.

Pastor Joe had some work he wanted to complete before everyone got there, so he arrived at the church an hour early.

It was late fall and already the sky was turning dark. It

The Power House

was even darker that evening, due to a storm that was forming in the west. Pastor Joe was walking across the lawn from his car, going towards the church. The wind was beginning to blow, and the sky was looking ominous.

From around the corner of the building came a man, staggering and clutching something to his chest. He stumbled as he started to turn the corner.

Pastor Joe ran to the man to assist him. As he approached the man, he could tell that something was definitely wrong with him. He had an unkempt appearance, and Pastor Joe could smell alcohol, as he reached out to help him up from where he had just fallen.

The man stood upright and stepped away from Pastor Joe, with a menacing look on his face.

That is when Pastor Joe looked closer at the man in the darkness and saw that he had a gun pointed at him.

Pastor Joe could feel his heart beating faster and the blood pulsing in his neck, causing a roaring in his ears. He had never experienced anything like this in his life, and he was frightened by the look on the man's face.

"Well, if it isn't the almighty preacher himself!" exclaimed the man.

"I can't believe it, here you finally are, all by yourself. How could I get so lucky?" he sneered at Pastor Joe.

Pastor Joe stepped back in alarm.

The man said, "Just stand still there, Preacher, until I tell you to move."

He ran his hand over his face that showed a two or three day growth of beard. He seemed to be trying to clear his eyes, and his senses.

Then he looked up at Pastor Joe and said, "Git in your office and don't act like anything is going on if we meet anybody on the way."

Pastor Joe said, "Sir, I don't know what your problem is, or why you are here, but I would be glad to talk to you about anything concerning you. You don't need that gun, I can assure you."

"Just shut your mouth and git in that church, Preacher. That's all I hear from you is talk, talk, talk. Always that *goody two shoes,* talk, talk, talk."

Pastor Joe was confused, because he was certain he had never met this man before.

Then, he realized that the man might possibly have seen him on the Sunday morning telecast on one of the several television stations on which his sermons were shown, tape delayed.

He also realized the man was very drunk and was not in control of himself at the moment. He exhibited signs of great agitation and the propensity for violence.

Pastor Joe could feel this in his spirit, and he knew he was in grave danger from this man.

He stepped slowly toward the man and said, "It's okay, it's okay. I will go with you. But let's go through the back in order to avoid anyone that might be coming through the front."

"Sounds like a good idea to me," said the man, as he stepped behind Pastor Joe, pushing him forward with the barrel of the gun.

As he walked to the study, Pastor Joe began to pray, asking God to help him.

His heart began to beat a little slower, and he took some deep breaths, praying as he opened the door of the study.

The man shoved Pastor Joe into the study and quickly slammed the door behind him, locking it. Then, he turned and motioned Pastor Joe to a chair.

He went behind the desk and sat in Pastor Joe's chair. He leaned back and put his mud caked shoes on a stack of papers that Anna had placed there that afternoon, in readiness for the meeting. He took out a cigarette and lit it, with one hand, blowing smoke all over the room.

The Power House

Pastor Joe sat very still, not taking his eyes from the man who continued to point the gun at him.

The man reached in his overcoat and drew out a pint of whiskey. He took a long drink from the almost empty bottle, then, threw it against the wall, smashing it to pieces.

Pastor Joe flinched as tiny pieces of glass flew all over the room, leaving a ghastly smell of alcohol in his study.

He held his breath, not knowing what to expect next.

"Preacher, let me tell you something!" the man shouted. "You think just because you have a church and a big congregation, and because you are on television every Sunday, that you rule the world. You think you can make all the rules, and that you have all the answers, don't ya?"

"Well, don't ya?" he yelled as he stood up and slapped his hand on the desk.

Pastor Joe said, as calmly as possible, "No, I don't rule the world and I don't have all the answers. It's true that I preach and that I have a large congregation and a program on television, but it's all due to the glory of God, none to me."

"There you go, see what I mean?" shouted the man. "All the answers and the glory to God," he repeated mockingly. "Well, let me tell you where the glory to God has left me, Preacher," the man raged.

"It has left me without my wife and my two little boys. And all because of your preaching about the glory of God and the sin of alcohol and men supposed to be this or that."

"My wife started watching you on television on Sunday mornings. Then, when I told her to turn that junk off, she secretly started taping it on Sunday's and watching it when I went out with the boys after work for a drink."

"Oh, yeah, she thought she was real smart, but I found the video, and she admitted it, after I smacked her a few times," he said smugly.

Pastor Joe was now getting the picture, loud and clear. He saw the type of person he was dealing with. He imagined the wife, looking for answers and seeking a better life, from his sermons.

"Where is your wife now?" asked Pastor Joe.

"Well, you tell me!" exclaimed the man. "You the man with all the answers ain't ya?" he shouted at Pastor Joe.

"Last I heard, she was in the place you people set up for run away wives. You the one would know where she is, and I intend for you to go git her outta there, and I'm goin' with ya," he said with a sneer.

"You got a lotta nerve trying to bust up families like that. You stand up there on Sunday morning and talk about how God wants to keep families together and the devil wants to bust them up. Well, what does that make you then, Preacher? The devil himself as far as I am concerned," he said.

He walked closer and pointed his finger in Pastor Joe's face as he said the part about the devil.

"It was all that gibberish you was preachin' that made her leave me. Don't believe me? Just look at this!" he shouted.

He pulled a letter from the breast pocket of his dirty overcoat.

"Read it, Preach, read it!" he yelled.

Pastor Joe leaned forward and cautiously took the letter from the man. It had been wadded up and straightened out many times.

"When did you get this letter?" asked Pastor Joe.

"Stop asking questions and just read the letter!" shouted the man.

Pastor Joe cleared his throat and looked at the letter that was stained with tears as it was being written.

"*Dear Warren,*" read Pastor Joe.

"*I have tried to talk to you, and I have tried so many times to tell you that I can't live like this anymore. I can't stand to see my kids raised in a house with you. Warren, I have told you and told you that I have found the Lord. You won't hear it. You won't believe it. But, after hearing Pastor*

Joe last Sunday morning, I knew in my heart that I had to get these kids away from you once and for all."

"You beat Josh when you came in drunk last Saturday until he wasn't able to move. You would have beaten Andy too, if you hadn't passed out. And I wouldn't go to church on Sunday with a black eye, so even though you were passed out from the night before, I didn't sneak out with the kids and go to church like I have been doing."

"I sat there in our house and I listened on the television. Pastor Joe spoke about how a man is the head of the household and should set an example for his children. That he should love his wife as Christ loved the church."

"He said how men that beat their wives and abuse their children are wrong and that they need to be prayed for. He prayed a prayer right then to change the hearts of those listening."

"Warren, I have prayed for you for so long. It hasn't done a bit of good."

"I am taking these kids out of this house you call a home and we are going to have a better life, no matter what it takes."

"Don't try to find me, it won't do any good. I am not coming back and neither are these kids. They are afraid of you and so am I."

"I finally realized that I was doing them more harm by trying to stay and be a family than leaving. If we stayed, they might not live to grow up, much less have a chance at a decent life."

"I will keep praying for you, but God will have to change your heart a lot.

And even if he does, it won't matter, because I am not coming back."

"Goodbye, Stella."

When he finished reading the letter, Pastor Joe looked up, expecting to see a sad face, or at least tears in the man's

The Power House

eyes. All he saw was cold hatred. Hatred for Pastor Joe and hatred for Stella for leaving him.

It was unnerving to Pastor Joe, never having had to deal with such hostility before. He waited to see what Warren planned to do next.

Warren picked up a stack of papers from Pastor Joe's desk and slung them across the room.

"Alright, almighty Preacher, git up and let's go get Stella," said Warren.

"My neighbor told me she came to your church for help last Sunday evening. He wasn't gonna tell me, but I could tell he knew, so I shot him with this pistol I have pointed right at you."

Pastor Joe flinched, imagining Warren actually shooting a man with the gun he had pointed directly at him.

"After I shot him, his wife decided it *might* be a good time to tell me," Warren said, with a sinister laugh. "I have been staked out behind the church since then, watching for you. So, don't go thinking I won't use this gun on you, too. Now, let's go fetch my wife and kids," he said, reaching for Pastor Joe's arm.

Pastor Joe pulled his arm back and said, "I am sorry, but I cannot do that, Warren. I will not endanger the lives of your wife and children, and all the others, if she is there."

"Well, we will see about that," said Warren, waving his gun in the air.

He stumbled towards Pastor Joe, tripping on an electric cord that had been run from the lamp to the wall. As he fell, the gun fired accidentally, shattering the computer screen on Pastor Joe's desk.

Anna was coming down the hallway just as the gun fired. She stopped and waited for a moment. Then, she heard glass shattering. She couldn't believe what she was hearing. She ran to the pastor's study and began banging on the door, calling out to Pastor Joe.

The Power House

Warren regained his balance and stood up again, pointing the gun at the pastor.

"Tell her everything's fine in here. No, better than that, go open the door and tell her to come in here," he ordered Pastor Joe.

"I won't do that," said Pastor Joe. "Please, just leave her out of this," he begged Warren.

Warren kept the gun pointed at the pastor while he eased the door open, standing slightly behind it, just out of Anna's sight. She cautiously opened the door wider, entering when she saw Pastor Joe sitting there.

As she crossed the threshold, Warren stepped from behind the door and pulled her in, slamming the door behind her, locking it. Anna screamed when she saw the gun pointed at Pastor Joe.

"Shut up, will ya?" said Warren.

"Pastor Joe, are you alright?" asked Anna, her voice shaking.

"I'm fine," Pastor Joe assured her.

"I said shut up! Now git over there and sit down," demanded Warren.

Anna crossed the floor on wobbly legs and sat on the sofa behind the chair, where Pastor Joe sat very still. Very frightened, she looked at Pastor Joe.

"Pastor Joe, what's going on?"

Warren started ranting, again, about how it was the pastor's fault that his wife and kids had left him. He threw the letter at Anna. She read it quickly, then, realized that she knew who this man was.

She had greeted his wife and children when they came to the church earlier that week seeking help.

She was the one who took them to the Eagle's Wings Shelter for Battered Women.

She recalled the black eye the woman had, and the bruises on the face and arms of the small boy she carried in her arms.

So, this is the man who caused all the pain to them, she thought. *No wonder they ran away from him.*

There was no remorse in the man. There was no repentance for what he had done. All he wanted was to have his wife and children back so he could control them.

Pastor Joe found himself wanting to ask Warren if he would let him pray with him about the situation. Then, he felt a check in his spirit. He knew the Lord was warning him not to say that. He knew it might be the final *"straw that broke the camels back"* with Warren. He sat still and waited to see what Warren would do.

"Well, now it seems I got me a little leverage," Warren finally said.

"Either you git yourself up and go with me to git my wife and kids, or I will put a bullet through this lady's head. Do we understand each other?"

Pastor Joe jumped up from his chair and said, "No, no, don't say that. Don't even think that, please. Leave Anna out of it, she doesn't have a thing to do with this situation."

"Anna, is it?" said Warren. "Well, Miss Anna, then maybe *you* know where my wife and kids are, huh, since you work for Preacher here?"

He looked at her and she noticed Pastor Joe standing behind him, shaking his head for her to say "no."

She said in her heart, *God forgive me for lying*, then, said, "No, I don't know where your wife and children are."

Warren started forward, angrier than ever.

"You are lying in church," he said, lunging at Anna.

As he reached to grab Anna by the shoulder to shake her, Pastor Joe knocked the gun from his hand, sending it skipping across the room, like a rock across the still water of a lake. He pushed Warren away from Anna, and as he did, Warren fell and his head hit the side of the desk, knocking him out cold.

Pastor Joe shouted to Anna to call 911, but Anna had already begun talking to the emergency operator, telling them to send help.

Pastor Joe went to the side of the room where the gun lay, picked it up, and gingerly put it in his jacket pocket. He didn't like anything to do with guns; however, he was afraid that if Warren woke up and out muscled him, he might get the gun back again. He couldn't allow that to happen.

When members of the church began showing up for the meeting, they were surprised to see police cars with their lights flashing in the parking lot of the church.

They were asked to wait outside.

In a few moments, policemen emerged from the church with a dazed, drunken man, shouting at the top of his lungs, "It ain't over, Preacher. It ain't over. I'll get Stella and those kids back."

But, it *was* over, for Warren Graves, at least. After his arrest, he was charged with two counts of assault and battery of his wife and children. He was charged with threatening to kill Pastor Joe and Anna.

He was also charged with *murder.*

When the police arrived, they revealed to Pastor Joe and Anna that Warren Graves was wanted for murder.

He had told Pastor Joe that he shot his neighbor. The neighbor had died two days before and they had been searching for Warren Graves since the time that the shooting was reported by the man's wife.

When Anna heard that Warren had already killed a man, she began shaking and crying. Pastor Joe put his arm around her to comfort her.

He had felt in his spirit that Warren Graves was a violent man. He now knew to what extent he would have gone to get his wife and children back.

Pastor Joe shuddered at the thought.

Thank you, God, for your mercy, he thought.

The Power House

Warren Graves was sentenced to life in prison. His wife and children were free of an evil man whose heart would not change. A man with no respect for human life.

It was a frightening experience for Pastor Joe and Anna, but once again, God turned evil to good.

A shaken, but relieved, Pastor Joe and Anna left the courtroom, and thanked God for their lives, and for the release of the lives of the woman and her children from the evil of Warren Graves.

The news of the incident at the church traveled fast and people talked about what had happened there for weeks on end.

After the trial of Warren Graves and his being sentenced to life in prison, things soon became normal again.

Stella Graves got a divorce from her abusive husband and changed her name back to her maiden name, Stella Kavanaugh.

She began taking her children to church on Sundays, and was hired as a permanent employee at the Eagle's Wings Shelter for Battered Women.

She was a tireless and compassionate worker at the shelter. She could relate to what she saw there, and was willing to go beyond her job description to make sure the women and children who came there received love and care.

She spent many nights sitting up with children that had been brought in, while a physician attended the wounds of their mothers, inflicted by their fathers.

She would never forget how the Lord had brought her out of that, and was a good witness about God's mercy to the women who came, seeking shelter, and peace in their lives.

CHAPTER ELEVEN

After things settled back to a normal pace, Eva suggested to Pastor Joe they take a vacation. The boys were both in high school and could manage on their own. Besides, Anna was always there to look in on them. Pastor Joe agreed that it would be a good thing to have some time away for just himself and Eva, so plans were made for a vacation for the two of them.

Eva was to bring home brochures for ideas of where they would go, and Pastor Joe agreed they would look over the brochures and pray about where God would lead them.

One evening, Eva came home with twenty-three brochures she had picked up at the travel agency. She put them on the counter in the kitchen and started cooking dinner.

Pastor Joe came in an hour later and picked up the brochures. He had gone through about a dozen of them, when he came across one showing a huge statue of Christ with the slogan, *"If I Be Lifted Up, I'll Draw All Men Unto Me."*

It was a beautiful picture.

It showed an enormous, all white statue of Christ, standing over a mountainous area. The mountains were a panorama of different colors of leaves on the various types of trees. There was a waterfall cascading down the side of one of the mountains.

When Pastor Joe saw that particular brochure, he knew in his heart this was where he wanted to go. He saw Eva looking at him, with a smile on her face.

She shook her head, saying, "Me, too. That's the place that touched my heart when I saw it. Would you like to go there?"

Pastor Joe put the brochure back on the counter and went to put his arms around his wife.

"That's enough confirmation for me, sweetheart. And the sooner the better," he said. "Let's have a second honeymoon."

Eva was glad to hear the excitement in his voice about a vacation. It had always been difficult to get her husband to take time for just the two of them, because he felt such an obligation to his flock.

Now, he was showing enthusiasm for the trip she wanted so much in her heart. A trip for just the two of them, in the mountains with waterfalls cascading down the side.

Eva, herself, was always very involved with the church. She led an intercessory prayer group for the women. She had acknowledged her gift of intercession by the Lord years before.

Her spirit of discernment was very strong, and she spent countless hours ministering to the women of the church and those in the community.

Being a pastor's wife was anything but easy, but Eva found it very rewarding, and wouldn't change a thing about her life with Pastor Joe and their ministry. She thanked God daily for her husband, her children, her home, and most of all, for her Savior.

She was a bright, devout, fun-loving woman, and she and Pastor Joe were truly a match made in heaven.

"Don't forget to leave a note for Anna to remind her about Joey's soccer practice on Tuesday," said Eva, as they were getting ready to leave for their trip to the mountains.

"Already done, it's on the frig," said Pastor Joe.

"Did you get the small black suitcase from beside the bed?" asked Eva.

"Got it already, it's in the car," said Pastor Joe.

"Well, then I guess we can leave."

They locked the front door and began walking slowly towards the car, each trying to think if they had left something undone.

All at once, they looked at one another and started laughing at the same time. They began to race each other to the car, like two teenagers.

They were excited about their trip, and all of a sudden, could not wait to get there.

Their plane would be leaving in an hour and a half, and they didn't want to miss it. This was going to be a wonderful trip.

As they got in the car, as they always did, they continued to hold hands as Pastor Joe asked God to grant them safety, to watch over the children and the church. Then, he started the car, and they were off to their well-deserved vacation.

The hotel was old and quaint, with marble staircases and mahogany railings.

There was a huge balcony that looked out over the mountainside. The balcony had white wicker chairs, where people sat enjoying fresh, homemade lemonade, and the view.

Standing on the balcony, they could see the statue of Christ, standing with arms outstretched, seeming to preside over the entire area with His love and protection.

It was truly a magnificent sight.

To make things even better, Pastor Joe and Eva discovered an old convent on the grounds, where there were acres of roses growing, being tended by the hotel grounds crew.

Eva always teased her husband about his rose garden.

The Power House

She would tell him that he loved roses even more than she did. He had thirty something varieties. She had lost count.

The first evening there, they walked through the twilight, holding hands, taking path after path, smelling the fragrance of the roses, along with the clear mountain air.

Pastor Joe had talked to the concierge when they arrived, and found there was a famous chapel in the area, made of glass and wooden beams. It stood on the opposite side of the mountain, overlooking a beautiful meadow.

There were hiking trails behind the chapel, and Pastor Joe and Eva planned to go hiking after visiting the chapel the next morning.

Pastor Joe had reserved the Bridal Suite, and when Eva entered the room, there were her favorite red roses in a vase by the canopy bed.

Eva was very pleased with all the thought her husband had put into their *second honeymoon*.

When she sat down on feather bed, she noticed something on the pillow.

She reached over and picked it up. It was a small box with an envelope taped underneath it.

Eva looked questioningly at her husband, but he just smiled and said, "Open the box first."

She opened the box, and in it was a beautiful pendant. It had three roses on it. One rose was yellow gold, one white gold, and one rose gold.

She loved it immediately, and pinned it on her collar. Then she opened the envelope.

It was a poem that her husband had written for her. The poem read:

"*I knew the day I met you I could love only you.*

I knew the day I married you our love would be ever true.

The yellow rose is for our love that only continues to grow.

The white rose, for your heart, my love, as pure as driven snow.
The red rose is for the passion that wells inside of me,
For you, my precious Eva, the best wife that could ever be."

It was signed, *"With all my love, Your Joe"*.

Eva cried when she read the poem.

She felt that he truly cherished her, and that she was blessed to be his wife.

The next morning they arose, bright and early. They wanted to get to the chapel in time to watch the sunrise.

They each caught their breath at the beauty before them. The architecture of the building was magnificent. They could tell that, even in the dark before dawn.

They entered the chapel, noticing only one other person there, a woman, sitting at the very back.

They went past her, expecting her to look up, but she kept her head down.

They went to the front of the church and sat on the first pew, waiting for the sunrise.

They were not disappointed. The sun came slowly up over the mountain, across the meadow, spreading a soft, then bright light.

Suddenly, it shone on the meadow, revealing the array of glorious colors of the wildflowers there.

Eva and Pastor Joe sat there for over an hour in total silence, each with their own prayers and their own thoughts.

As they rose to leave the chapel, they noticed the woman still sitting in the same position in the back row. She had her head lowered, however, she did not appear to be praying, she was staring straight ahead.

Something rose up in Eva's spirit, a "something", that she knew from years of experience, was discernment. She felt drawn to talk to this woman.

She looked at Pastor Joe and motioned him to go on

The Power House

ahead and wait outside.

He stepped out of the chapel, as Eva eased into the seat beside the woman.

"Good morning, I hope I am not disturbing you," said Eva, smiling at the woman.

"No, you aren't disturbing me, Ma'am," said the woman.

"I noticed you when my husband and I came in to watch the sunrise. Wasn't it just beautiful?" asked Eva.

"Yes, it was. I come here about once a week to see the sun come up. It's one of my favorite places to think."

She was very somber, very shy, not returning Eva's smile. Eva noticed a distant look in the woman's eyes and a sadness she could not hide.

"My name is Eva DuPriest. My husband and I are on vacation. We heard about this chapel from the concierge at the hotel and wanted to see it for ourselves. He mentioned the hiking trails behind the chapel. We are going hiking in a little while."

"It's nice to meet you. My name is Sarah. I live about five miles from here. I can see why people are always wanting to come here. I come because is it so beautiful and so quiet, and it gives me time to think."

Eva said, "My husband is a minister and we don't have a lot of quiet time, except for our prayer time. It is nice to have this time to slow down."

"A minister?"

"Yes, and, Sarah, I hope you will understand this when I tell you that the Lord put it on my heart to talk to you this morning. I don't know why yet, but if you will let me, I would like to pray with you."

"Well, Ma'am, if you want to pray with me, that would be fine with me."

"Please call me Eva."

"Alright, Eva, then let's pray."

Eva took Sarah's hand and started to pray.

"Dear Lord," prayed Eva. "Please be with us now, as we come to you, seeking wisdom and discernment for your will to be done in this hour. I pray that you reveal to Sarah, and to me, what you would have us pray for. You know the reason you put us together for this prayer. Thank you for your love, Lord. Thank you for your mercy. I pray that you will bless Sarah and that you will meet whatever need she may have. I ask this in Jesus name."

She did not add the *"amen"*, waiting to see if Sarah wanted to pray.

Sarah started praying, thanking God for Eva's obedience in stopping to pray with her. Her voice was very low and timid. She said a brief prayer, then, grew quiet again.

Eva sat still for a few moments, but did not feel any discernment in her spirit as to why the Lord had asked her to pray for this woman. Eva finished her prayer, stood, and removed her hand from Sarah's.

"I pray God will bless you, Sarah and meet your needs, whatever they may be."

Eva turned to leave the chapel, but felt that she could not yet go. A strange force compelled Eva to turn around and go back to where Sarah was standing. She placed her hands on Sarah's shoulders, facing her. It felt as though there were magnets drawing her hands there, keeping them on Sarah's shoulders.

All at once, Eva felt a sorrow well up within her soul. A sorrow like she had never known. It came over her like a fog. It felt as though someone had kicked her, really hard, in her stomach. Her chest was aching; there was a severe pain underneath her breastbone. She found herself sobbing, uncontrollably. She heard herself wailing, felt tears covering her face. Still, she could not let Sarah go.

The sorrow was overwhelming, the pain intense, and very real. Sarah just stood there staring at Eva, with a concerned look on her face.

Eva finally pulled Sarah back down on a seat and said, "Sarah, I feel such an overwhelming sorrow. All I know is that this sorrow has to something to do with you. I don't understand it. But, Sarah, somehow I know that you do."

For a moment, Sarah didn't speak. Then, she shook her head in an affirmative manner, and lowered her head.

"Please tell me what it is about, Sarah, or it's going to literally kill me," pleaded Eva.

Pastor Joe had glanced in to see Eva bending over, holding her chest, and crying very hard. He started quickly towards the door. But, the Holy Spirit stopped him. He turned and went to the car to wait on Eva, knowing the Lord was using her to do His work, as He did so often.

Sarah let out a small sigh, then, took both Eva's hands in hers. As she did, she began to cry as loudly as Eva had been crying. Sobs tore through her, gut wrenching sobs.

Eva stopped crying, just as Sarah began. She sat and rocked Sarah, like a small child, until she regained enough composure to speak. That took over ten minutes.

"It's about my David, my son," said Sarah. "That's what this is all about. He died in a car wreck two years ago and I haven't even cried about it."

"I have just felt stunned for years. I know that he died. I went to the funeral. But, I haven't talked about it, and until now, I haven't really felt anything, except numb, since it happened."

All at once, her tears began to flow, and Sarah began to wail, loudly.

"Oh, God! Oh, God! It hurts, it hurts," cried Sarah.

Sarah doubled up, sitting on the bench, rocking herself back and forth and crying, with a broken heart. She put her hands in her hair, holding her head, continuing to rock back and forth.

Eva rubbed her softly on the back, until Sarah finished the story of the car accident that killed her son, at the age of

The Power House

fifteen, two years before.

Ten more minutes passed, and Sarah began to look at Eva, really look at her.

She began growing calmer and was able to speak without sobbing.

"That's what God wanted to do, isn't it, Eva?" Sarah asked. "He used you to make me to deal with this, after all these years. That's why He allowed you to hurt, like I should have hurt, after I lost David."

"Yes, I believe that has to be it," said Eva.

"I am so sorry you had to feel what I just felt. But, as funny as it may seem to you, I actually can say it's just good to feel *something* again."

She laughed softly.

She reached out her arms and hugged Eva.

Eva was praying the entire time that God would give Sarah peace now and let her get on with her life. She could not imagine Sarah having to feel that much sorrow ever again. She knew *she* certainly didn't want to feel that kind of pain ever again.

As they stood to go, Sarah asked Eva for her last name, and where she could get in touch with her. She told her she was going to go see her husband at his work to let him know what had just occurred in the glass chapel on the mountain. He had been extremely concerned about Sarah these past years, since their son died.

After giving Sarah the information she wanted, and a last hug, Eva stepped outside, wiping her eyes from the emotional battle she had just experienced. She went to the car to find Pastor Joe waiting for her.

When she got in the car she said, "Joe, honey, I think hiking will have to wait until tomorrow. I am totally exhausted."

Then, she told him what had happened and how the Lord had once again used her.

"I must say, I am so glad Sarah was able to have that breakthrough, but I hope I never have to experience pain like that. Joe, it was so terrible."

She started crying again, thinking about the sorrow that the woman had to deal with over the loss of her son.

And, it hadn't come until two years after the young man had died. Then, God chose Eva to help the woman deal with her loss.

"Hiking can wait. Let's go down and have a big blueberry pancake breakfast and see the antique shops. You need a break, sweetheart."

He leaned over and kissed Eva on top of the head.

"Thank you, Lord. We are your servants, and after all my years in the ministry, you never cease to amaze me," he said in prayer. "Please give Sarah your peace that passes all understanding. And, thank you, Lord, for putting Eva in her path."

He started the car and they headed down the mountain in the direction of the quaint little village below.

They spent the rest of the day in the village, shopping in the antique stores, and having lunch at a small English tearoom with a patio built out onto the side of the mountain. The patio had a fountain in the center of it. A cool breeze blew leaves across the patio.

Pastor Joe and Eva sat on chintz covered chairs, sipping their tea on the patio, enjoying the lovely fall day.

They talked about when they first met, when Pastor Joe was just *Joe* going to seminary and Eva was still in school, studying photography.

She said, "Joe, we have seen some wonderful places here to photograph. Some day, I would like to come back here with my equipment and take some pictures."

"Consider it done, Eva. God willing, we will come back the same time next year for what the natives here call the *flaming fall review*."

The Power House

"It's a date," said Eva, and reached up to touch her husband's hand that he had just pressed to her cheek.

He grabbed her hand and said, "Come on, little darlin'. I see a kid's swing underneath that tree over there. You get in the swing, and I'll push you."

Eva laughed as she ran along beside her husband, happy that God had given him such a healthy zest for life.

CHAPTER TWELVE

Pastor Joe was preaching on Sunday morning the following week. The church was practically filled to capacity. As he took his place at the podium, the congregation stood and began to applaud. He felt like it was a hero's welcome and actually felt a bit embarrassed by the ovation he was receiving.

The love shown by his congregation really touched his heart. "Praise God from whom all blessings flow," he began. He held his hand up to quiet the congregation.

"Eva and I just got back last night from the most wonderful vacation. I want to thank all of those who pitched in to do the things we normally do around here, so that we could get away. Bless you for your time and for the love you all have shown us. It is good to be back in the House of the Lord."

He heard at least ten *amen's* from that comment. Then he began his sermon.

The sermon was on the gifts of the spirit. It seemed to be a fitting subject, after the experience Eva had with Sarah in the glass chapel on the mountain.

The sermon was well received by the congregation and many people came to the altar to give their lives to Christ, vowing to use the gifts He had graciously given them.

The Power House

It is wonderful to be back in God's house, winning souls to Christ, thought Pastor Joe as he received the new believers at the altar.

That afternoon after lunch, Joey came in to visit with his parents and hear more about their trip. They had gotten in late the night before, and he had not had an opportunity to talk with them.

Paul, their oldest son, was upstairs, studying for a calculus exam, so he wouldn't be down for awhile. Joey had something he wanted to tell his parents.

Joey had a friend named Charlie Williams, who had a little sister named Savannah. Savannah was five years old.

Charlie's father was a traveling salesman and was gone most of the time.

For several weeks Charlie, his mother, and Savannah all had what seemed to be a case of the flu. They all seemed sluggish and sick at their stomach most of the time.

Charlie did not feel as bad as his mother and Savannah did, so he did most of the shopping and errands that needed running. It seemed all his mother and Savannah wanted to do was sleep.

One night, Charlie and Mrs. Williams were watching television in the den. Charlie's mother was lying on the sofa, and Charlie was sitting at the other end.

Savannah had been in bed most of the afternoon, and it was now well into the evening, and she was still sleeping.

All of a sudden, Savannah came into the den and started staring at the wall above the television. She began smiling and nodding her head "yes."

She said, "Oh, Mommy, Charlie, look at the beautiful lady. Look at the beautiful colors!"

Then, as they watched her, she shook her head again and said, "Okay."

They turned and looked at one another, wondering what in the world was going on with Savannah.

The Power House

Charlie's mother turned off the television set and said, "Savannah, honey, come here."

She pulled her up onto her lap. She brushed her hair back, felt her head to see if she had a fever. That would explain her seeming to be having hallucinations.

She was cool as a cucumber.

Charlie's mother said, "Savannah, who were you talking to just now?"

Savannah smiled and said, "A beautiful lady with wings that had all different colors. The lady smiled at me and said, "Savannah, don't you worry. You are going to be alright. That's when I said, "Okay."

Charlie and his mother still just looked at one another, wondering what this was about. Savannah was not the type of child to make up stories. But, here she was just waking up and saying she saw a *lady with wings* on the wall above the television.

Charlie got up and went to look above the television.

Then, he turned to his mother and said, "Mom, there's a thing up there on the wall. I think it is the carbon monoxide detector."

Charlie's mother took a deep breath and had a puzzled look on her face. They had the detector installed only months before.

She wondered if something was wrong with the detector.

The next morning Mrs. Williams called the gas company to send someone to come out and test the house for carbon monoxide. When the man brought the meter in, the needle went off the charts. The house was filled with carbon monoxide.

The man from the gas company went around opening windows immediately, asking Mrs. Williams if anyone in the house had any symptoms of carbon monoxide poisoning. She explained to him how she and her children had been sick for weeks, always feeling sick at their stomachs and sleepy.

"It's a wonder you didn't die," he said, "with the levels of carbon monoxide so high in here. You need to get to the doctor and get checked out to make sure you are all okay. I just checked the detector, Ma'am, and the unit is defective and couldn't possibly have gone off. How in the world did you figure out to call us, anyway?"

She explained to him about what had happened the night before, about Savannah seeing the *lady*. He stood there for a few minutes, just looking at her with a strange expression. Then he shrugged his shoulders and turned to open another window.

Mrs. Williams was now convinced that it had been an angel that Savannah saw. An angel that saved their lives. She and Charlie were now calling her *Savannah's Angel*.

Mrs. Williams insisted that Charlie come with them to the doctor's office. The doctor checked all three of them, and pronounced Charlie healthy. However, he gave oxygen to Mrs. Williams and Savannah to clear their lungs, just in case. He said he would feel better if they received oxygen.

Mrs. Williams called her husband, Robert, the minute she got home from the doctor, to tell him what had occurred. Together, they thanked God for saving her life, and the lives of the children. They thanked Him for sending *Savannah's Angel*.

"Can you believe that? Charlie just told me at church this morning what happened. I couldn't wait to tell you and Dad," he said to his mother.

Pastor Joe and Eva were on the edge of their seats in the living room, as they listened to Joey tell the story of what had happened while they were away.

Pastor Joe told Joey, "I want to ask Mrs. Williams to give a testimony before the church about what God did for their family. Also, do you think Charlie would talk to the youth group tonight and tell them the story? Not only do we want to give God the glory for sending *Savannah's Angel* to save *their* lives, but other people may heed this as a warning as well. I think we should all double check our carbon monoxide detectors and smoke alarms."

"Well, they were so thankful, Dad, and so happy that God saved them. I know they plan on being at church tonight, because Charlie and I are going to take two of the girls from the group out for pizza afterwards. I can go call him now, if you like. Then he can ask his mom while I have him on the phone," said Joey.

"That's a great idea," said Pastor Joe. "Your mom and I will wait here while you go call. And, Joey, thank you, son, for sharing that story with us. Isn't God good?"

"All the time!" shouted Joey as he ran to make his phone call.

He returned in a few minutes to tell his father that the entire Williams family would be at the service that evening, including the father. They would gladly share their recent experience with the congregation.

The following week, Robert Williams was going to interview for a job that did not involve traveling. The travel involved with his job kept him away from home the majority of the time.

The incident that just occurred with his family had made him stop and think about his priorities, and he knew there was a double message here from the Lord. It was something that had been on his heart for quite some time, and this only confirmed his feelings.

Charlie was a teen-ager and Robert had already missed so many of Charlie's activities, like the soccer games, and his junior prom night. He didn't want to miss anything involving his family ever again. Savannah was only five. There would be many activities for her, dance recitals, soccer games, school plays. He planned to be there.

He had already talked to Gina, his wife, and she agreed that if they had to economize and tighten the budget, until

The Power House

he was promoted in the new job, then they would do whatever was necessary.

A new job for Robert that did not involve travel was what Gina had been praying for. But, she knew it had taken the Lord to change her husband's heart. Robert loved his job, and was very successful.

Of course, there was much more that she did not know about the message her husband received from the Lord through this incident. She was about to find out what that message was.

That night after church, Robert came to Gina in the living room, where she was sitting, reading her daily devotional. Charlie was out with Joey and two girls from their youth group having pizza. Savannah was already in bed.

"Gina, tonight was a real turning point for us. We have never stood up in church and talked before the entire congregation. Especially to give a testimony. It's funny, but I think that is the most rewarding speech I have ever given. I have to speak all the time, as you know, in a sales capacity. But, this was different. I know in my heart that the Lord arranged all this, including the part about me changing jobs."

Gina closed her devotional, laid it down on the table beside her and removed her reading glasses.

"You know, Robert, I have been praying that God would change your heart about your job. I know you love what you do, but the kids and I need you here. I am so glad you came to that same conclusion. I want to thank you, honey for making that decision. I know it is a sacrifice for you to leave the job you have had for ten years, especially when you are doing so well."

Robert listened to what Gina said. Then, he took on a somber look.

"While we have some time alone, Gina, I feel I ought to confess some things to you."

Gina became very quiet, almost afraid of what Robert

might say next. Like most wives of traveling salesmen, Gina had anxious moments about him being on the road, with all the temptations out there in the world. She wanted to trust Robert, but there were times when nagging doubts would pursue her. She couldn't stop thinking those thoughts, when he was away from her and the children. She had always prayed her way through those times, but the thoughts occasionally would reoccur.

Gina sat very still, not saying a word, waiting for Robert to speak again.

"Two years ago, I started going to the bar in the hotel after work, when I had someone traveling with me," he began.

Gina sat up a little straighter at hearing those words from Robert. She could not imagine her husband going into bars. It just did not fit the image she had of him. She had never known him to even take a drink.

"Well, at first all I did was drink tonic water with lime," said Robert. "Then, one of the guys caught on and had the bartender put vodka in the glass, along with the tonic water and lime. I have to say, I couldn't really tell the difference in the taste of it, because they kept me talking while we drank. Then, all at once everything became brighter, and everyone became funnier. Finally, they confessed that they had pulled a practical joke on me."

"But, the next time we all went to the bar, I found myself wanting to laugh like we had that first night, for things to seem brighter. It had been a really hard day, raining, flights delayed. So, I found myself ordering a vodka tonic, with lime, along with the rest of them. Gina, I have been drinking while I was on the road for two years now," said Robert.

"You never knew it, because I never drank around you. And, that wasn't difficult, either, because I haven't been home that much."

Gina looked at Robert with a frown starting to appear

The Power House

across her forehead. She could not believe what she was hearing, from the man she thought she knew.

"That's not all, either," said Robert, clearing his throat.

He noticed Gina lean farther back in her chair.

"I know you aren't pleased with what I am telling you, and neither am I. I am ashamed that I ever took that first drink. Not the one the guys gave me. The one I ordered for myself."

Robert stopped and put his face in his hands, rubbing his palms up and down on his cheeks, then over his eyebrows. Self-consciously, he put his hands in his lap, and Gina noticed that his fists were tightly clenched. She was very sure, at this point, she wasn't going to like the rest of the conversation any more than she had the first part. She was right.

"About six months ago, I went into the bar with Gerald after work. He got a page, and left to make a business call from his room. Normally, I only went to the bar with the guys, and would have gotten up to leave when Gerald left. But, it was a really hard day, and the liquor was starting to relax me, so I just stayed. There was a woman sitting at the bar, laughing with the bartender. Her name was Doris."

At the mention of a woman, Gina's spine stiffened.

She really didn't want to hear the rest of his confession, but, in her heart she knew she must.

"Well, anyway, the bartender was the one that helped the guys pull the joke about the vodka with me on my first drink. He had been telling the woman about what happened and that now I was a regular when I was in town. That was what they had been laughing about."

"She got up and came over to my table, drink in hand, and said, "Well, I see we have something in common. I drink vodka and tonic, too."

"I just sat there for a minute, like a bump on a log, and then I said something like, "Good stuff, helps me out after a hard day."

The Power House

"She just stood there for about fifteen seconds, looking at me with a smile on her face."

"Finally I said, "Would you like to sit down?""

Gina leaned back and took a deep breath. She had no idea what Robert was going to tell her.

"Well, anyway," continued Robert. "She said, "Sure, thanks. My name is Doris.""

"Then, she shook hands with me. She told me she was in town for a convention and that all her friends had gone out to a dinner theatre that evening, to see a new play in town. She said she was too tired to go, after sitting in the convention all day, and besides, she had already seen the play."

"Then, she signaled the bartender to bring us some more drinks. "

"I guess we sat there talking and drinking for three hours, at least. Gerald told me later that he stuck his head in the door to see if I wanted to grab dinner, because he had already called my room, and I wasn't there. He said he saw I was having a good time, laughing and all, so he went on and had dinner by himself."

Gina sat there, tears forming in her eyes, wondering what was coming next.

"I got up to leave, to go back to my room. I could tell I had too much to drink, when I stood up, because I stumbled into a chair."

"Doris laughed, then, took my arm when I was trying to leave and said she really liked me and would like to see me again."

"I said, "Thank you, I like you too.""

Gina was the one who put her head in her hands this time.

She couldn't look at Robert. He could tell that she was swallowing the lump in her throat.

"Gina, it had been so long since I had been home - that month I had to spend in Baltimore on that seaboard project, remember? I know it isn't any excuse. I was flattered to have that much attention, plus the fact that I was drunk."

"I went over to pay the bar tab, and when I reached in my billfold, a picture fell out. It was the one we all had made at the company picnic last year, the one of you and me, and Charlie and Savannah, all with baseball bats."

Robert swallowed hard, then, tears appeared in his eyes, as he thought of the picture. He continued.

"I looked at that picture, and, all of a sudden, the drunken fog lifted from my brain. I looked up and saw myself in the reflection of the mirror behind the bar and couldn't believe that was really me. It made me sick at my stomach to think I had sat in a bar drinking with a strange woman for three hours, with you sitting here with the kids, by yourself at home."

"Gina, I threw a fifty dollar bill down on the counter and ran out of that bar. I never even looked at the woman, when I was leaving. I went straight to my room, and I got on my knees and I begged God to forgive me."

He paused, looking at Gina.

"I thought that would be the end of it, but the next week, I found myself wanting another drink. Found myself wanting to find a bar. I didn't realize it, and I couldn't believe it, but I had gotten addicted to alcohol in that two year period, since I took that first drink."

Gina found that she could not say one word. She just sat there listening to her husband's confession, wishing she had never heard the first word of it. She still couldn't look at him.

He made no move to touch her. He knew by her body language that would be a huge mistake, at this point. He needed to finish his story.

"Three months ago, when I was in St. Louis, I went to my first AA meeting. I didn't want to go there. I wanted to go to the bar. I found myself driving around in the rain, wanting to go into every bar I saw, with lights flashing outside, seeming to welcome me in."

"Instead, I found myself driving through dark streets. Then, all of a sudden, I realized that I was out of the bar area and into a neighborhood. I turned a curve, and there was a big Catholic church on the corner, with people coming out. But, the lights were still on, so I knew there would be someone there."

"I stopped the car, got out, and went in to find the priest. I found him right in the hallway, when I entered. He took one look at me, knew he had never seen me before, and since they were having committee meetings instead of church that night, knew that I was there because I was in need of something."

"He came over to me and asked how he could help me. I asked if we could go somewhere we could talk privately, so he took me to his office. He sat beside me on a bench and listened to my problems."

"I told him everything, Gina. From the first drink, to the part about the woman, and the picture falling out of my billfold, as I was paying the check."

"Then, he said, "Son, it is a good sign that you came here tonight. The Lord led you here, do you believe that?"

"I told him I *did* believe it. I told him how far I had fallen away from the Lord. Well, he said there was an AA meeting in the basement of the church that very night, it would be starting in twenty minutes. Can you believe that?"

Robert just shook his head, still in disbelief of what had happened that night, three months before.

"He prayed with me and then led me down the stairs to the meeting. He told me to take the first step on my own, then, he left me."

"When I got there, I saw about fifteen people already in the room, and they all greeted me like a long-lost friend. By the end of the evening, there were about thirty people, altogether, I guess. I got up and told my story to strangers. I think it was probably easier on me that way."

"Well, I have been going to AA meetings every night, when I have been on the road. The first thing I do is look one up in the yellow pages, when I get into town. I will continue to go to the meetings until God assures me I don't have this problem any longer, no matter how long it takes."

Robert held his fist in the air to emphasize his dedication to that vow.

Then, he spoke softly to his wife.

"I know this is hard for you to hear, Gina. I hope you will believe me that I didn't do anything more with the woman than talk, and that I have never been back to that bar again. I won't ask for your forgiveness, because I know am putting a lot on you right now."

"I just hope you will understand what a shock it was to me to hear about the carbon monoxide and realize I almost lost my entire family. And, how grateful I am that God saved all of you. Funny, but I was in the process of being saved by Him myself."

Robert hung his head.

"It made me stop and think about what is important in this world. It's you, Gina. It's the kids. It's our family. It isn't being on the road making a lot of money, furthering my career. It's too high a price. It has cost us already more than I was ever willing to pay. All I can say is that I am truly sorry."

"I have prayed and asked God to forgive me. I have promised Him I would do all I can to be the head of this household and to be a better father to the children. I have failed all of you. I won't fail you again, with the help of the good Lord. You deserve the best, Gina, and I love you I want to be the best husband and father that I can be. But, whether you allow me to do that now is up to you."

Robert stopped talking at that point. He sat with his head down. He was rubbing his hand against his knee, nervously, waiting for Gina to speak.

The Power House

They heard Charlie coming in from his pizza date, calling goodnight to them, then, going up the stairs, whistling. At least someone in the family had been enjoying their evening. It certainly wasn't Gina or Robert.

Gina got up and stood for a moment, looking down at Robert.

"I am going for a walk," she said. "I will be back later."

She got up to leave. All Robert could do was watch, as she walked out the door, without looking back.

It had only been an hour, but the time seemed to drag for Robert, as he waited for Gina to come back home from her walk. He stayed in the living room, waiting and praying that God would soften her heart enough to forgive him and give him a second chance.

He heard her come in the front door, locking it behind her. Gina turned and saw that the light was still on in the living room. She knew Robert would be there, waiting on her. Waiting for what she might have to say.

When she entered the room, Robert looked up, but didn't move from the chair in which he was sitting.

Gina looked at him and said, "Robert, I want to say this one time and then we won't speak of it again."

He was frightened by the calmness in her voice and the seriousness of her tone.

"Robert, I have loved you for years. I loved you before you ever noticed me in our history class in college. I loved you the moment I set eyes on you. I loved you through the problems you had finding a job right out of college, and all the good times, and hard times since then. And I still love you, even after what you just told me about the woman. That's the part we won't speak of again."

"One thing I realized as I was out walking is that God gave all of us a second chance when he sent *Savannah's Angel*. He gave all of us a second chance when he sent us Jesus, our Savior. If He can do that for us, why can't I do that for you? We both know we all face temptations every day we are in this world. I am fully aware of what you must have endured out on the road, trying to make a living for our family. And, Robert I know that *nobody* is immune to temptation, especially when they are under the influence of alcohol."

"The devil never ceases to try to destroy families, Robert. You hear Pastor Joe preach on that same subject quite a bit. But, honey, it wasn't any coincidence our family picture fell out when you were paying that bar bill."

"God put that in front of your face to remind you of who you are. You are a husband and a father. Most of all, though, you are His, Robert."

"You belong to a God who *loves* families. You don't belong to the devil who tries to *destroy* them."

"You are a good man, and together, we will make our family stronger. I will help you with your drinking problem, if I can. I don't understand enough about alcoholism to do much about it right now, but I am willing to find out what I need to, in order to help you."

Robert had not moved from his chair since Gina had begun speaking. He waited on her to finish.

"And, let me say this," she continued, as she held up her hand.

"It may seem very strange to you, but I appreciate your telling me about what happened. I believe you when you say it stopped at talking. I believe you are truly sorry and that it won't ever happen again."

"And, even though you didn't ask me for my forgiveness, because you didn't feel you deserved it, I guess, you have it anyway. I forgive you, and I love you. I always have, I always will."

Then, she stepped forward and walked into Robert's outstretched arms.

Robert sobbed, as he realized the depth of the love his wife had for him, from her words of forgiveness. Their home would once again become a home of love and laughter.

God had not only saved their lives, He saved their family. He caused Robert to see how much they meant to him and how he could have lost them in a moment's time.

Robert rejoiced in his soul that he had not lost them due to the carbon monoxide. He rejoiced that he had not lost them due to a foolish act on his part, while he was under the influence of alcohol.

He was thankful he had listened to what God was telling him in his heart that night he stopped at the Catholic Church in St. Louis.

Across town, Pastor Joe and Eva were saying their evening prayers. They were thanking God once more for saving the Williams family. They just didn't know the extent to which they had been saved.

CHAPTER THIRTEEN

Families were very important to both Eva and Joseph Dupriest. Right now they were concerned about their own family. It looked as though there might be some problems with their oldest son, Paul.

The week they were gone to the mountains, they had called home one evening and Joey had been there alone. Brett was working that night, and Anna and David Joseph had just left, after bringing over some Chinese food to share with the boys.

Paul was supposed to come home at seven o'clock for dinner with Joey and Anna every evening. However, he had not come home for dinner two nights in a row.

They had asked Joey what time Paul finally came home on those particular nights, but he said he didn't know. He had gone to bed at ten-thirty, as was usual for him on a school night.

When Paul came in from school that day, Pastor Joe and Eva were waiting to talk with him.

He came in the back door, patted their dog Sparky, and then came into the kitchen.

Eva was standing by the sink, and Pastor Joe was sitting at the counter.

"What's up?" he said nervously as he grabbed an apple from a bowl on the counter.

"Since when did you start addressing your parents with *what's up*, Paul?" asked Pastor Joe.

"Sorry, I didn't mean to be disrespectful. Everybody says that at school, and it just slipped out."

He looked at Eva with a questioning look on his face.

"We wanted to talk to you, Paul, about the fact that you didn't come home for dinner like you were supposed to for several nights while we were out of town," began Eva. "We should be the ones asking you *what's up,* don't you think?" she asked.

Paul took a deep breath and with a frown beginning on his face, turned around to put his jacket on the hook behind the kitchen door.

"Who said something, Joey, or Mrs. Anna?" asked Paul.

"Neither," said Pastor Joe. "We called home to talk to both of you boys and you weren't here either night. We decided to wait until tonight to ask you to explain why you weren't home at the time you were supposed to be."

Pastor Joe indicated to Paul to sit at the counter beside him.

"Son, you know that we understand you have friends. But, you also understand our family rules. When we make plans for you to be at home at dinner time with your brother, then that is where we expect you to be," said Pastor Joe.

"Yes, Sir, I know. I'm sorry."

"That doesn't answer our question. Where were you and why weren't you home on time?" quizzed his father.

Paul became very quiet, cracking his knuckles, looking at the wall above the sink.

"I had planned to talk to you both tonight after dinner," said Paul. "I was going to talk to you last night, but when I came down from working on my calculus homework, Joey was talking to you about the thing with Charlie and his family, so I decided to wait."

"I was out with some new friends I met at school," said Paul, finally after a few moments. "We went down to the bowling alley and hung out. Then, they wanted to go riding around after the bowling alley closed, so I went along with them."

Pastor Joe said, "Paul, the bowling alley closes at eleven-thirty. What time did you get in?"

Paul cleared his throat. He was not accustomed to having to answer these types of questions, because he usually did exactly as he was expected to do. He was very uncomfortable.

"It was around one-thirty the first time, and around two the next time," he said.

"Oh, Paul, surely not!" exclaimed Eva. "What on earth were you doing all that time, Paul? And, especially on a school night."

"We went to some girls' house and toilet papered her yard," he said.

"A couple of the guys were mad at her and said her father would really give her grief if it ever happened again. I guess they had done it before and really made him angry."

"Well, I have toilet papered yards before, when I was a kid, too, but it was usually because we liked the girls that we did that, in my day," said Pastor Joe. "But, we never did it at one-thirty or two in the morning."

"Well, there's even more to it than that, Dad," said Paul.

He shifted nervously on his stool.

"Okay, here it is. We went to Wal-Mart first and Tim went in and stole the toilet paper. The rest of us waited outside in the car."

"I thought he was going to buy a big bunch of toilet paper. I didn't know he was stealing it, until he came back to the car, bragging about it. Anyhow, the guys I was out with that night were mad at the girl, because she turned them in for smoking pot behind the school during lunch break."

Eva and Pastor Joe both drew in a deep breath at Paul's confession.

"Oh, no, Paul, you weren't smoking pot?" Eva said anxiously.

"No, Ma'am, I wasn't. I never have smoked pot and I have never tried any kind of drug, either. They keep trying to get me to, calling me *Preacher's Kid* and all, but I haven't ever done it."

"Then, if you know how these boys are, why are you running around with them?" asked Pastor Joe.

"Well, they are the coolest guys in school. All the girls hang out around them. They make it seem like everything they do is a lot of fun."

"But, that night, when we went over there to roll the house, the girls' little sister saw us, when she got up to go to the bathroom. She went and got her father and he called the police. The guys were all smoking pot that night, and had some beer in the car."

Pastor Joe and Eva just looked at one another, unable to believe what their oldest son was telling them.

"When the police car started up the street with the lights flashing, Randy jumped in his car to try to get away and he was blocked off and arrested. He was stoned and drunk when they took him down to the station. The rest of us ran in the woods behind her house. They didn't catch us."

"I thought they found out who we are and that's what this was about, when I came in just now," said Paul. "I was hoping I would have a chance to tell you before you found out."

"No, we didn't know anything about it, until you told us," said Pastor Joe. "Paul, how could you be involved in such a bad situation?"

"I have been asking myself the same thing for days, Dad. I kept thinking about it, thinking I should just go ahead and tell you and Mom."

"The second night, the rest of us that got away the first night met behind the bowling alley after it closed. I didn't stay the whole time. I came and sat outside in the swing in the back yard, until I knew Joey was asleep."

"I didn't want to answer any questions from him. I fell asleep and woke up about two and went on in the house then."

"I haven't hung around with those guys since that happened. I know I made a bad choice in friends. Their character wasn't even questionable. It was obvious."

"But, that one time of nearly getting in serious trouble was enough for me, believe me. It scared me real bad. Somehow, running around with those guys has lost its appeal for me," said Paul. "Most of all, I am sorry I let you both down."

"No, Paul, you let yourself down when you did that," said Pastor Joe. "You have been taught from the time you were a small child to avoid situations like that. My question for you to pray about is whether you would have continued to run with those guys, if you hadn't almost gotten caught. They weren't just doing something bad or obnoxious. They were doing something totally illegal. More than that, though, it is sinful in the eyes of the Lord. And so were you, by being involved in it. You know that, don't you, Paul?" asked Pastor Joe.

"Yes, sir, I do know that. I never was comfortable with what they were doing, but it felt good to be included in the popular bunch. As long as we were at school, everything seemed okay. I can see now how wrong I was," Paul said, as he hung his head.

"Paul, you know how much Joey looks up to you. What would he think of you, if he knew you had compromised your Christian ethics and standards this way?" Pastor Joe asked.

Paul's eyes widened at the thought of letting Joey down.

His eyes misted when he said, "I think I have to tell him. I think I need to let him know how easy it is to get sucked into such a situation. Besides, Joey is more trusting than I am. It might happen to him easier than it did to me. I couldn't stand to see that happen."

"If you feel that strongly about it, as Joey's brother, how do you think we feel about it being your parents?" said Pastor Joe. "But, at least you are willing to admit your mistakes."

Paul sat quietly at the counter, waiting on his father to deal out his punishment.

"I think that talking to Joey is a good idea, and I am glad you offered to do it. I would like you to tell him in a family conference this evening. Then, I want you to be in the house every night by dinner, and you are to go nowhere, other than school and soccer practice, for two weeks."

"Paul, you pray about what you think a fitting punishment would be for you, and at the end of the two weeks, I want you to tell me what the Lord has told you about it. Is that agreed?" said Pastor Joe to Eva.

"Yes, that sounds fine," said Eva, turning to the kitchen sink and taking out the sprayer, making motions to clean the sink.

Eva was very hurt. She wiped her eyes on her apron, still finding it difficult to believe that her oldest son would do something so dreadful. He was one of the strongest members of the youth group at church. He was one of the best players on the soccer team.

He has loved the Lord all his life, and now this? she asked herself.

She felt so disappointed that her son had any involvement in stealing, smoking, drinking, trespassing and vandalizing someone's property.

He may not have stolen, but he was in the car. He may not have smoked pot or drank any beer, but he stayed there when he knew the others were smoking it and drinking. At least, he admitted what had happened. It was difficult for that fact to console her at the moment.

She turned and went upstairs, without looking at Paul or Pastor Joe. She went immediately to her side of the bed, and knelt to ask God's forgiveness for her son, and to pray that he would not ever be a part of such a thing again.

As she knelt beside the bed, she caught a glimpse of Paul's picture sitting on her dresser. It was a picture of Pastor Joe and the two boys she had taken the day Pastor Joe baptized both of them.

She took the picture and held it next to her heart, as she prayed for her sons.

"Dear Lord, I pray with a mother's heart, please, hear me. How well I know that we live in a world where two forces pull against one another. I know the exposure my sons have had to the world, which is full of temptation and evil ways. I know in your word it says, *"Greater is He who is in me than he who is in the world."* I also know the exposure they have had to your word, since they were tiny babies. Paul came to know you at such an early age."

"Dear Lord, please draw him back to you and let him see the error of his ways. Please forgive him, as I will. Lord, please be with us tonight in our family conference. Give him a heart of repentance and the words to say to Joey about what he has done. Lord, help Joe and me to say and do the right things, as parents, in this situation."

"You know that we forgive him, as you tell us to do, but we also know we are responsible for guiding this child in his youth. That he must be made responsible for his actions. Be with us, Dear Lord, in this home tonight and let us all know your will. In Jesus name I pray. Amen."

Eva rose from kneeling by her bed. She went into her bathroom and washed the tearstains from her face. She started downstairs to make dinner. She passed Paul's room and even though the door was closed, she could hear him praying, as she had been.

The Power House

She knew in her heart he was sorry for what he had done, and she was just glad it had stopped at the point it did.

She knew it was not a coincidence the little sister had gotten up during the night and had seen the boys in the yard.

She felt God had been in this all along, watching over Paul. Otherwise, things might not have stopped with the two evenings he went out. She shuddered to think of some of the stories she heard from women who came to her for counsel and solace, from the errant ways of their children.

It was very quiet at the dinner table that evening. Joey kept looking at his parents, wondering what was wrong. As soon as dessert was finished, Eva announced there would be a family conference in the den when the dishes were put in the dishwasher. Joey offered to help his mother, wanting to find out beforehand what was the reason for the conference.

When Pastor Joe and Paul left the room, he said in a worried tone, "Mom, what is going on? What are we conferencing about? Everything okay with you and Dad?"

"Everything is fine with us health wise, if that is what you mean. It's just that something has come up concerning the entire family, and it needs sharing. Come on now, and help me finish the kitchen, so we can go sit down with your father and Paul," replied Eva.

When they reached the den, Paul and his father were sitting across from one another. Pastor Joe was on the sofa, Paul on the loveseat. Eva sat beside Paul, so that Joey would sit beside his father, facing his brother. Nobody said anything for a minute, the parents waiting for Paul to begin.

Paul looked at each of them, then, deciding they wanted him to start, began to talk.

"Joey, the reason we are here tonight is because of me. Remember last week when Mom and Dad were out of town and I didn't come home for dinner, like I was supposed to?" he asked his brother.

Joey said, hesitatingly, looking at his parents, "Uhhh,

The Power House

yeaaah, I remember."

"Well, the reason I didn't come home for dinner is because I was out doing things I shouldn't have done," Paul said.

He then told Joey the entire story. He told him about getting involved with the wrong crowd at school. About Tim stealing the toilet paper. About his participation in rolling the house and Randy's getting arrested.

Joey sat there, with his mouth open and his eyes widening, all the time Paul talked. Joey could not believe what he was hearing. Paul had always been his hero. Paul was the outstanding soccer player, while Joey struggled just to stay on the team. Paul was the straight A student, while it was all he could do to keep a B average.

Paul was the youth leader, who always admonished the others when they got out of line, telling them they should remember to ask themselves, "What Would Jesus Do?"

He was having a difficult time believing Paul would do such things. Then, he looked at his mother and father, knowing what they must be feeling. He felt a strange knot forming in the pit of his stomach.

"Joey, I am the one who decided to tell you just what kind of trouble I have gotten myself into," said Paul. "Mom and Dad didn't force me to do this. I just think you need to know how easy it is to let other people influence you. I don't blame those guys. I blame myself. I acted out of pride, wanting to be with the popular crowd."

"There is this one girl that I have been trying to get to go out with me. And, she wouldn't, because she said I was a *Preacher's Kid,* and I wouldn't be any fun. She is in that crowd, and to tell you the truth, that's the reason I started hanging out with them."

"I know, now, that I really don't want to date her, anyway. I found out that she does drugs, not just smoking pot either. When she heard I went out that night and almost got into trouble with that group, she came up to me the next night at the bowling alley and asked me to take her riding. Just the two of us, to have some *real* fun. She was high on something. When I stepped back and looked at her, I couldn't believe how ugly she seemed to me, all of a sudden."

"Joey, it hit me all at once, the stuff I had done the night before, and the reality of the situation sunk in. I got in the car and came home. I stayed out in the swing in the backyard, until you turned your lights out. Then I guess I fell asleep. I didn't make it into the house and into bed until two a.m."

"Joey, I hate what I did. I have asked God to forgive me, and I have said that I am sorry to Mom and Dad. But, I need to tell you how sorry I am, too. I have really let you down. I ask you to forgive me, too. And, Mom and Dad, I want to say this here and now. I am proud to be a *Preacher's Kid* and to know I belong to the Lord, not to the world."

With those words, he started to cry. He hadn't cried like that since his grandfather, Eva's father, died several years before.

Eva and Pastor Joe went over, along with Joey, and knelt by their son. They put their arms around him until he stopped crying. Then, they told him they forgave him, and that they were proud of him for being so straight forward with them about what had happened. But most of all, that he made the right choice in the end. Their *raising up a child in the way he should go* had paid off.

Pastor Joe and Eva left the room, leaving Joey to talk with his brother. When they reached their bedroom, they put their arms around one another, rejoicing that their son had done the right thing. They were proud of Paul. They were grateful for his honesty, and that tonight he showed signs of becoming the man they always prayed he would become.

Eva went downstairs to the den after everyone else in the house had gone to bed. She turned on a reading lamp beside her favorite chair. She put the Bible in her lap.

Not having any particular passage in mind, she casually opened the Bible and let the Holy Spirit guide her. As she looked down, her eyes fell on Psalm 32.

"Blessed is he whose transgression is forgiven, whose sin is covered. Blessed is the man to whom the Lord does not impute iniquity and in whose spirit there is no deceit. When I kept silent, my bones grew old through my groaning all the day long. For day and night your hand was heavy upon me; my vitality was turned into the drought of summer.

I acknowledged my sin to you and my iniquity I have not hidden. I said, "I will confess my sin to the Lord"—and you forgave the iniquity of my sin. For this cause everyone who is godly shall pray to you in a time when you may be found; surely in the flood of great waters, they shall not come near him. You are my hiding place; you shall preserve me from trouble. You shall surround me with songs of deliverance." Selah

Eva read on, knowing this was what the Lord had led her to read about her son, Paul.

"I will instruct you and teach you in the way you should go; I will guide you with My eye. Do not be like the horse or like the mule, which have no understanding which must be harnessed with bit and bridle else they will not come near you.

Many sorrows shall be to the wicked, but he who trusts in the Lord, mercy shall surround him. Be glad in the Lord and be glad, you righteous; and shout for joy, all you upright in heart!"

"Thank you, Lord, for the reading of your word. Thank you, Lord, that my son has asked forgiveness of his transgressions. Not only of you, but from our entire family."

"I understand your word tonight. I understand that while he was keeping quiet about what had happened, it was actually eating away at him. Praise you, dear Lord, that Paul remembered your word and that you watched over him. Thank you for showing him the truth about what he was doing."

"Thank you that he is not defiant or like the horse or mule having to be controlled. Thank you that you have given him a strong spirit and a strong mind for reasoning your word."

Reading the last verse again, she began to softly sing, *"My Jesus, my Savior, Lord there is none like you. All of my days, I'll sing the praises of your righteous love. My comfort, my shelter, tower of refuge and strength. Let every breath, all that I am, never cease to worship you. Shout to the Lord all the earth let us sing. Power and majesty, praise to the king. Mountains bow down and the seas will roar at the sound of your name."*

Eva stopped singing, then closed her Bible and thanked God for her family.

CHAPTER FOURTEEN

Pastor Joe was up early the next morning. He had to complete some of his work before noon because he was teaching classes at the seminary three afternoons a week. He was about the leave the house when the telephone rang.

It was Stephen Wells, one of their members at the church. Pastor Joe could tell from Stephen's voice that something terrible had happened.

"Just take a deep breath, Stephen, and calm down. Tell me what is going on."

"Pastor Joe, it's our youngest daughter, Chloe. She was kidnapped from the bowling alley last night. Could you please come over here and be with us?"

"Dear Lord, Stephen, I am so sorry to hear about Chloe. But, please don't lose faith. We just pray that God will return Chloe, safely. I will ask Eva to start the prayer chain, and I will be over to be with you and Angela, as soon as I can get dressed," said Pastor Joe.

"God bless you, Pastor Joe. We really do need you here right now," said Stephen.

The shock of what Pastor Joe told Eva about little Chloe being kidnapped tore through her like a knife.

She could only imagine what Angela must be feeling.

She called the first person on the prayer chain, and knew that, within an hour or two, there would be hundreds of people praying for the return of the child.

She dropped to her knees in the kitchen, after putting the telephone back in the cradle. She had heard many stories lately on the news about children being kidnapped. Many of the stories had very sad endings. All she knew to do was pray that this one would turn out better for the Wells family.

"Dear Lord. Oh, Dear Lord. Please see fit to spare that child. Please, Lord, help them find her. Bring her home safely to Angela and Stephen. Lord, you know where she is. Please be there with her. Comfort her with your spirit."

"Little Chloe knows you, Lord. She will be praying to you herself, but, I pray this with a *mother's* heart."

"Please be with Angela and Stephen during this difficult time, Dear Lord. Give them the grace to face the situation. Lord, please bring their child back to them. In Jesus name I pray this, Dear Lord. With a *mother's* heart, I ask this. Amen."

Eva wiped the tears from her face, then, went upstairs to hug both her children.

Pastor Joe knelt with the Wells family in the living room of their home, leading them in prayer for Chloe.

Across the entire town, people were receiving telephone calls from the prayer chain and were bowing their heads in prayer, asking God to send the child home safely to her parents.

After they finished praying, Stephen told Pastor Joe, step-by-step, what had happened leading up to Chloes' disappearance.

Carly, the oldest daughter, sat in the window seat, staring out the window. She listened to her father telling Pastor Joe the details of the day before. She sat, remembering what had happened.

Carly Wells couldn't wait to go to the bowling alley that

The Power House

Thursday evening. It wasn't that she liked bowling that much. She knew James Tremont would be there for his bowling league, as he always was on Thursday nights. Her mother's voice pierced through her daydream about James.

"Carly. Please come down here for a moment. I need to talk to you," said Mrs. Wells.

"Be right there, Mom," yelled Carly.

She laid her hairbrush on the dresser and started down the stairs. As she neared the bottom, she saw her younger sister, Chloe, jumping up and down and clapping her hands.

"Oh boy, oh boy!" said Chloe in an excited voice.

"Carly, there you are," said Mrs. Wells. "I need you to take Chloe with you tonight, to the bowling alley."

As Carly started to protest, Mrs. Wells held up her hand and said, "I know, I know, you don't want to feel like you are having to drag your little sister along with you everywhere you go. But, tonight you will just have to take her, or stay at home with her. Your father and I have a counseling session with Dr. Conrad this evening. I am hoping we can find some way to resolve our differences. Wouldn't you like to see us all be a family again?" she asked Carly.

"Oh, alright, I'll take her with me," said Carly. "You know I want to see you and Dad get things worked out between you. I wish he would come home. It's only been a couple of months, but it seems like a year since he left. I really miss him, Mama."

"Well, maybe he will want to come home, if we can get some resolutions to the things that are bothering him," said Mrs. Wells. "I plan on going to work at the florist, as soon as school starts. That should help ease the finances. I know he has a lot on his mind right now. He can't seem to take the everyday stress of living with us. Thanks, Carly. It really helps me for you to take Chloe with you. We can't afford a sitter, and I really need to go to this session tonight."

"Okay, but you owe me," said Carly, with a teasing

The Power House

smile, to her mother.

"Get your jacket, Squirt, it's a little chilly out there this evening," said Carly to Chloe.

They entered the bowling alley, and Carly immediately began looking around for James Tremont.

There he is! Oh, he is soooo cute, she thought, excitedly, as she shrugged off her jacket.

"Come on, Chloe, let's go watch James bowl."

Chloe let Carly lead her to the far side of the bowling alley where James and his bowling team were just starting their first frame. She sat for awhile, watching the boys take their turns at bowling.

Carly waited patiently for them to finish. When they finished the first frame, James came over to where she and Chloe were sitting.

"Come on you two and I'll buy you something to drink," said James.

He reached out and mussed Chloe's hair. She gave him a big smile. She liked James, too.

"Carly, I need to go to the restroom," said Chloe.

"Can't you wait until we have something to drink, Chloe?" asked Carly.

She looked at James, rolling her eyes at him.

"No, I really need to *go*. But, it's ok; you don't have to go with me. I can go by myself," suggested Chloe.

"Chloe, you know Mama said you always have to stay right with me," said Carly.

"I'll be fine. Look," said Chloe, pointing towards the ladies room that was only twenty feet away. "It's just right there."

"Oh, alright, go ahead. But, hurry up and come right back here when you get finished."

Chloe started to the ladies room and Carly turned to talk to James. He wanted to tell her about something funny that had happened after gym class that day in school.

She became engrossed in his story, and only after she laughed and said, "I'm glad Chloe wasn't around to hear that," did she realize that Chloe had not come back from the ladies room. It had been over ten minutes since Chloe had left her.

"Excuse me a minute, James. I have to go check on Chloe," said Carly.

Carly got up from the seat in the lounge area and went to the ladies room. She looked around, but there was no sign of Chloe. She checked each stall, calling for Chloe all the while. Still, no Chloe.

She stepped outside the ladies room and began looking around. She didn't see Chloe anywhere. She went back to where James was sitting.

"She's not there," she said. "Mama is going to kill me, if I don't find her in a hurry," said Carly. "She is always telling me not to let Chloe out of my sight. After all, she is only ten years old."

Together, James and Carly looked for Chloe. When they didn't find her, they went to the security guard, who was standing at the front door.

"Have you seen this little girl tonight?" asked Carly, showing the security guard a picture of Chloe that she kept in her wallet.

"Hmmmn," said the security guard, rubbing his chin. "Oh, yeah," he finally said. "I saw her leaving about five minutes ago."

"Leaving?" said Carly frantically. "Did you say *leaving*? Leaving with who?"

"She was with a tall guy. The only reason I paid any attention is because he kept bending down to hear what she was saying. I thought it was funny that she didn't talk louder so he wouldn't have to bend down so far."

"Oh, dear heavenly God!" said Carly. "James, we have got to call Mama. Where's the phone?" she asked the security guard, beginning to panic.

"Over here, right over here, come with me, I'll show you."

He began to walk over towards the pay phone that stood outside the office.

"What's wrong, what's the matter?" he asked Carly.

"She wasn't supposed to leave here with anybody. I am her sister, and she wasn't supposed to leave here with anybody except me," said Carly, starting to cry.

She dialed information to get the telephone number of Dr. Conrad's office.

Mama and Dad should both be there, she thought, as she dialed the number.

"Dr. Conrad's office is closed. Please call back during regular office hours. Our hours are eight a.m. until five-thirty p.m. If this is an emergency, please hang up and call the hospital ER, or dial 9ll," said the voice on the answering machine recording.

"Then, we just have to call the police," said Carly to James.

She dialed 9ll.

The police arrived within five minutes of Carly Well's telephone call. They began to take notes on what time Carly last saw Chloe.

They asked the security guard questions pertaining to times and to the description of the man with whom Chloe had left the bowling alley.

"I have got to reach Mama and Dad. Will you please take me over there? They are at Dr. Conrad's office near the hospital," Carly asked the policeman.

"Sure, Ma'am. Let's get going. Every minute counts in a situation like this," said the policeman to Carly.

"James, will you please stay here, in case Chloe comes back?" she asked.

"Sure, Carly," said James, patting her on the shoulder.

The Power House

"I'll stay until they close. If she isn't back here by then, I'll come over to your house. Okay?" asked James.

"Okay, thanks. Now, I have got to go," said Carly, as the policeman waved from the door, motioning her to hurry.

The policeman banged on the door with his flashlight. He finally was able to get Dr. Conrad to come to the front door of his office and let Carly talk to her parents.

Angela and Stephen Wells were not angry with Carly, as she had feared. They were only concerned with where their youngest daughter could have gone and who might have taken her from the bowling alley.

Carly was inconsolable. She was crying hysterically. Dr. Conrad took her into the other room to talk with her, while the police talked with her parents.

"We will put out an alert for anyone who has seen your daughter to contact the police station," said the young policeman, who was working the case.

"I will need a current picture of Chloe," he told Angela.

"Can you come by the house?" asked Angela. "We just had new photos taken and they are on the buffet at our house."

"I'll follow you home," he said.

That night was one of the longest nights the Wells family ever spent. A detective was sent over to be with the family. There was always the possibility of someone calling them for ransom. There was no way of knowing where Chloe was, or who might have taken her.

Stephen Wells spent the night in his own home for the first time in months, since his separation from Angela. They clung to each other, in fear for the life of their child.

The next morning, Stephen called Pastor Joe and asked him to come over and be with them.

As they prayed together, Angela and Stephen held onto each other for comfort. The differences they had been talking about with Dr. Conrad the evening before seemed so minute. They would have been embarrassed if someone had

The Power House

mentioned those problems to them that morning, in light of the tragedy they were now facing.

The telephone began ringing. Stephen Wells went to answer it. Angela stood beside Pastor Joe, biting her fingernails.

Douglas Coleman, the detective, came from the kitchen where he had been drinking coffee, waiting to see who might be calling.

"It's for you," said Stephen, to Detective Coleman.

"It's the police station," he said to Angela.

Douglas took the telephone from Stephen.

"I see. Okay, I will get everyone together and we will be right down," he said to the person who was calling.

He turned to Stephen and Angela.

"We have to go to the police station right away. The security guard remembered that they had a security camera at the door Chloe was leaving from. They have a video they want all of you to look at to see if you can recognize anyone. You need to hurry, the clock is ticking," he said, anxiously.

They all hurriedly got into the family van to go downtown to the police station. Pastor Joe went with them. The detective followed in his car.

Stephen and Angela Wells looked at the video footage. It wasn't a high tech camera, so the video was fuzzy. They did not recognize the man, but they recognized their little girl.

As Angela watched the video of Chloe walking away with the man, she began to sob, feeling the frustration of seeing her little girl being taken away by a stranger, and feeling helpless, and unable to do a thing to stop it. Pastor Joe placed his hand on her shoulder to comfort her.

They noticed that, as Chloe walked out of the bowling alley with the man, he was bending down to hear her speaking to him. There was no sound to the video. The man's face was turned away from the camera, so they couldn't see him.

Carly started to cry, then stopped, and stepped closer to the television screen.

"Could you please play it again?" asked Carly, wiping her eyes.

"Sure," said the policeman who was running the video.

He hit the replay button on the VCR. Carly stood for a moment, looking at the video. Something was very familiar about the man with Chloe. She couldn't see his face, but there was something that reminded her of someone. She couldn't think of who it was. She became very upset with herself, feeling that she should recognize the man. The frustration caused her to start crying again.

"That's okay, honey," said Stephen, putting his arms around Carly. "Maybe you will think of it later."

They were getting in the van to go back home, when all of a sudden, Carly drew a deep breath. She snapped her fingers, as she remembered.

She then shouted, "It's Donald Reeves!"

She got out of the van and ran around to her father, pulling at his jacket.

"Dad! Dad! It's Donald Reeves. It's Donald Reeves, the caretaker at Chloe's school."

"How do you know that, Carly? We couldn't see the man's face on the video. How can you be so sure?" asked Pastor Joe.

"Did you see the way he kept scratching his head with his left hand? Well, Chloe and two of her friends were at the house one day and they were laughing about the way he looked like the Laurel and Hardy guy that scratches his head like that."

"Chloe told them not to laugh at him, that she felt sorry for him. She said he was always wanting her to talk to him when she went out for recess."

"She pointed him out to me one day, when I went to pick her up at school. He waved at us and then, when he was walking away, he scratched his head like that. Chloe and I laughed about it, because I thought he really did look like the Laurel and Hardy guy," said Carly.

"Dad, that's him! I know that was him with Chloe! I know it!" she exclaimed.

"Alright, let's go back in and talk to the police," said Stephen, praying that Carly was right.

They all got out of the car and hurried back into the police station. They replayed the video, and watched as the man stood up straight after listening to something Chloe had said, then scratched the top of his head, with his left hand.

The police checked with the school. They found that Donald Reeves had taken the day off for a sick day - for the first time in four years.

Going on Carly's identification of Donald Reeves as the man who kidnapped her sister, and the fact that he had not missed a single day for the past four years, until today, they called in the S.W.A.T. team and surrounded his house.

They could see movement through the blinds in the front of the house that were partially closed. Someone was definitely in the house. They had to be careful, because they had to assume there was a ten year old child there, as well.

"Donald Reeves! This is the police!" came the loud call from the bullhorn.

"Open the front door, and step outside," said Captain Spears. "The house is entirely surrounded. Open the door and come outside NOW!"

In a few moments, Donald Reeves opened the door of his house and stepped onto the porch. He held his hands up, surrendering, like he had seen happen many times on the television programs he watched. He never said one word to the police when he was arrested. He did not resist the arrest.

Two policemen hurried to the porch and handcuffed him, while members of the S.W.A.T. team covered them.

Stephen and Angela Wells surged forward, but were

restrained by several policemen. Pastor Joe put his hand on Stephen's shoulder and prayed quietly.

He knew this ordeal was far from over. They still had to find Chloe.

"You have to wait until we have checked inside for your daughter," the policemen informed the couple.

One of them turned to take the document being handed him by a policeman who had just come on the scene. It was a search warrant. They couldn't afford to make any legal errors. They had seen this happen too many times. They wanted to have all their bases covered, in a case like this.

Stephen and Angela watched helplessly, as Donald Reeves was read his rights and led to a patrol car. They pushed the top of his head down, so he wouldn't hit the frame of the door as he got into the back of the car. He waited while the police entered his house. He sat staring blankly at Stephen and Angela from the back seat of the patrol car.

Sergeant Clay entered the house, along with Sergeant Kenworth. They had their guns drawn, in case there was someone else in the house that might cause them harm.

After they checked downstairs, Sergeant Clay motioned to Sergeant Kenworth to go upstairs, while he checked the basement. The basement door was locked with a padlock. Sergeant Clay went outside to the patrol car and asked to have Donald Reeves searched for the key. He could have shot the lock off, but if Chloe was there, he couldn't take a chance of injuring the child on the other side of the door. They found the key clutched tightly in Donald Reeve's hand.

Sergeant Clay took the key from his hand, then, went back down to the basement. He opened the door with the key, as Sergeant Kenworth covered him.

Chloe Wells was sitting on the floor at a coffee table. She had been crying. When she saw the policeman, she flinched and pushed herself backwards, grasping her knees

The Power House

with her hands, and pulling them close to her body.

Sergeant Clay had a little girl Chloe's age. He handed the gun to Sergeant Kenworth and knelt down where he was. He talked to Chloe from the doorway. He knew that the first thing the child needed was reassurance. His heart was in his throat, as he spoke to the child. He could see the terror in her eyes.

"Chloe, we are policemen. We came to take you home. You are safe now; nobody is going to hurt you. Chloe, your mother and father are right outside," he said softly.

Chloe sat there looking at both the policemen. She had a frightened look on her face. Then, grasping what was happening, she blinked and looked up at Sergeant Clay. She got up from where she was sitting and started slowly towards him.

He held out his arms and said, "You are safe now, honey."

Chloe began to sob, as she went into his arms. She was shaking violently, as she clung to the safety of the young policeman.

Two policemen were waiting with the Wells family. They were told to restrain them from coming in the house until the situation had been thoroughly checked.

Angela Wells had her eyes focused on the front door of Donald Reeves' house. When she saw Sergeant Clay coming out the door with Chloe in his arms, wild horses could not have stopped her from reaching her baby.

Angela was crying with joy, and Chloe was crying from relief, when she saw her mother. Angela tore herself from Stephen's grasp, eluded the policemen, and ran to throw her arms around Chloe. Everyone stepped back and left the two of them alone for a few moments. Then, Stephen joined Angela and Chloe.

Carly was still being restrained by the police, but when she saw her sister, she began crying and shouting Chloe's name. She was allowed to join the family reunion on the steps of the house.

Raising his eyes towards heaven, Pastor Joe said, "Thank you, Dear God. Thank you for returning this child to her family."

Pastor Joe stood beside the family, wiping the tears from his eyes. As each family member hugged one another, they began to rejoice and thank God for saving Chloe.

Sergeant Clay bent down, and patted Chloe on the head. With tears in his eyes, he gave her a wobbly smile and added his own, "*Amen.*"

Donald Reeves was charged with kidnapping and child endangerment. Chloe was asked to tell the police what had happened. She was willing, as long as her mother and father were right there with her, each holding one of her hands.

Donald had not harmed Chloe physically, other than pushing and shoving her. He kept telling the police that he only wanted her for his friend. She had befriended him on the school campus, when the other children laughed at him, and made jokes about him. She had shared her lunches with him and talked to him about her family.

He knew where they would be that Thursday night, because she had told him at school one afternoon that she was afraid Carly might be upset, because she was going to have to take her with her to the bowling alley.

Chloe had never been afraid of Donald, and that is how he had talked her into going outside with him that evening at the bowling alley. When she began telling him she needed to go back inside, she was speaking softly, and he had to bend to hear her. She was beginning to really be afraid of him, at that point.

Chloe was an innocent and trusting child. She had no way of knowing that Donald Reeves was mentally unstable. She found out, when he pushed her into the car at the bowling alley, and forced her to go home with him.

When she tried to reason with him that her family would be looking for her, he told her *he* was her family from then on. He pushed her into the basement, then, locked the door of the basement with Chloe inside. She began to sob, calling out for her mother.

Before Chloe's eyes, the man she had known as her friend became a raging, angry stranger. He held his hands over his ears and screamed at her to stop crying, then ran out of the room. In a few moments, he had returned with a kitchen knife in his hand and threatened to kill her if she didn't stop crying. He told her he had to leave the house for awhile in order to avoid harming her. At that point, Chloe became totally terrified of him, and did her best not to cry while he was watching her.

Everyone who heard the story knew how blessed they were that Carly had recognized Donald Reeves from the security video. Otherwise, there might have been an entirely different and tragic ending.

Stephen Wells realized the night Chloe was kidnapped how foolish he had been to leave his family. He asked forgiveness from his wife, and from his daughters for leaving them. He acknowledged that he had been weak in handling the financial situation, and the everyday stresses of life, and had literally tried to run away from the situation, and from them. He asked to come back home, so they could be a family again. Angela Wells welcomed him with open arms, as did Chloe and Carly.

It was a somber moment when the near tragedy was told by Pastor Joe on Sunday morning to the congregation at church. Angela and Stephen Wells wanted him to share their story, so that others might gain from their experience, and guard their children more closely.

They wanted to share their story, so that others might become more aware of the potential consequences of the innocence of an unattended, trusting child.

The Power House

Angela and Stephen Wells had learned a lesson from life, the hard way. They had thought, like many people do, that things like that happened to other people, not to them.

They would never think that way again. And, neither would Chloe.

CHAPTER FIFTEEN

Eva loved being a pastor's wife. It was a demanding role, sometimes it put her in the position of having to act as counselor and confidante to women in the church. She had understood what would be required of her as a minister's wife, even before she married Joseph DuPriest.

She thanked God for His gift of compassion and discernment that allowed her to help in counseling women with the problematic circumstances in their lives.

Reflecting on some of the situations she had heard of, she sighed, thinking how easy it would have been for things to have been even worse the night Paul was out with the boys. She was thankful he had seen the error of his ways before something so tragic happened with him.

All the temptations had been put before him. Stealing, taking drugs, drinking alcohol, illicit involvement with a girl, lying to his parents. He had been presented with choices that night, and he made the right choice on all, except his choice of friends. She knew he would be more careful from now on about the friends he chose.

She was right about that.

Several weeks later, Paul asked if he could bring home a girl from their youth group, for dinner.

The Power House

He was a high school senior, but he had not dated much. He usually went to group functions with other kids from the church.

Eva was surprised when he asked if he could invite a girl to dinner, however, she and Pastor Joe were happy to hear who it was.

They both knew Katherine and her family well. They had been original members of *the church with no name*, when it met in the community room.

Katherine was an outstanding young Christian woman. She and Pastor Joe couldn't be more pleased, and looked forward to having her in their home.

The following night, Paul was nervous about his date. He changed clothes two or three times. He put on ripped jeans and a t-shirt, then, decided it was too casual. He surveyed himself in a long sleeved shirt and dress pants and felt that he was too fancy, just for dinner at home.

Eva came upstairs and into his room.

"Mom, what do you think?"

He turned and showed her what he was a wearing, the shirt and dress pants.

"Too dressy," said Eva.

He pointed at the bed where the ripped jeans were lying with the t-shirt beside them.

"No way!" said Eva, as she laughed.

Paul laughed and threw open the doors to his closet.

"Help!" he said, as he gently pushed his mother inside the closet to find something appropriate. She emerged a few moments later with a white polo shirt and khaki pants.

"Yeah," said Paul. "That's the ticket. Thanks, Mom; you always know the right thing, don't you?"

"I try, sweetheart, I try. What time are you going to pick up Katherine?" she asked Paul, as she helped hang up the clothes he left on the bed.

"Six-thirty. I figured I would pick her up and we would

get back here in time to talk for about fifteen minutes before you put dinner on the table. Is that okay?"

"That's fine with me," said Eva.

"What are we having for dinner, Mom? I hope it's something she likes."

Eva raised her eyebrows at that one. He sure was going out of his way to please this girl. She was glad, though. That showed he cared about her.

"Roasted Cornish hens, wild rice, candied yams, and homemade rolls," said Eva. "I always heard you can't go wrong with chicken," she laughed.

"Yum," said Paul. "We haven't had your Cornish hens in awhile. I can't wait."

When Paul drove up to get Katherine, he found himself checking his hair in the mirror to make sure it was still lying down. He brushed the front of his shirt nervously.

Katherine opened the door when he rang the doorbell. Paul was relieved when he saw Katherine. He was glad he didn't have to sit around with her parents, waiting on her to come downstairs.

Of course, he already knew her parents, but it was different when he was there to pick up their daughter for a date. He would have felt a bit uncomfortable. He was glad that she had spared him the small talk. He was already nervous enough.

When they got to the car, Paul opened the door for Katherine, as he had been taught to do from an early age.

He went around to his side of the car and got in. He turned and looked at her as he started the car and said, "Katherine, you look great. I'm glad you are coming to our house for dinner for our first date. Uh, uh, I mean, well. I mean, I hope this is just our *first* date. I hope that we will have more."

He blushed, and she laughed.

"Paul, we have known each other for years. Don't be so nervous. I have to admit, though, that I hope this is just our *first* date, too," said Katherine. "I can't wait to see where you live, and I heard your mom is a really good cook. I know I am hungry. I skipped lunch today to help in the special education class."

If he had the courage, Paul would have told Katherine what he really thought about the way she looked. He would have used words like *incredible* or *gorgeous*. But, at the time, he was too shy to say what he felt.

Katherine had long, straight blonde hair and it was pulled back in a blue satin ribbon. She wore just enough makeup to make her blue eyes seem even brighter. She had on a simple, sleeveless, ankle length white dress that seemed to flow when she walked.

He felt his heart beating faster, as he looked at her, and he couldn't believe he had not noticed how pretty she was, until just a week before. It had taken him that long to get enough nerve to ask her out.

He was a little surprised that, when he asked her, she gave him a big smile and said *yes*, without hesitating. That she would love to go to dinner at his parent's house.

Katherine had liked Paul for quite some time. Most of the kids in the youth group already knew how she felt about him. She was friendly with everyone, so he never noticed the times she stared at him across the youth room, when they were doing skits, or singing songs. It had taken him a little longer to notice that there was something special about her.

She had a grace about her, the way she carried herself. He noticed that, as she got out of the car, when he opened the door. It reminded him of his mother. She was graceful like that, too.

"*Very becoming in a young woman*," he could just hear his father saying.

He gave Katherine a big smile, thinking about what his father would say, and took her arm, as they went up the front walk to the house.

"Dinner was wonderful, Mrs. DuPriest," said Katherine. "Let me help you with the dishes."

"Thank you, Katherine, but Joey and I are just going to rinse these and leave them for later," said Eva.

"You and Paul go on into the den with Pastor Joe and I will bring dessert in there. I left some pictures of our trip to the mountains on the coffee table, so you could see them. I am sure you heard Joe speak of our trip in church."

"I remember Pastor Joe talking about the trip you take every year on your anniversary. I would love to see your pictures of the statue and the chapel he talked about."

When they left the room, Joey said to Eva, "I never realized Katherine West was so pretty. She looks different tonight, doesn't she to you?"

"No, not to me," said Eva. "I have always thought Katherine was a beautiful girl."

"Youth ministry," said Katherine when the subject of college majors came up a few minutes later in the conversation.

"I have known from the time I was twelve years old what I wanted to be. The Lord called me to be a youth minister one Sunday night. I plan on starting to college as soon as the summer semester starts after graduation."

Paul looked quickly at his parents. He knew they were thinking the same thing he was. That was going to be his major, as well.

He cleared his throat and said, "Well, how about that?"

He had also planned on starting classes that summer after graduation.

"Well, you and Paul have a lot in common, then," said Eva.

"Oh?" said Katherine.

Paul filled her in on the fact that he had a calling, when he was thirteen, to go into youth ministry, and his plans paralleled those of Katherine's.

She was surprised. She knew he was strong in a leadership role in their own youth group, but she had no idea he had received a calling from the Lord, as she had, for becoming a youth minister. The idea of it made her smile. She noticed Joey looking back and forth at her and Paul, and smiling, too.

Paul had shared with their youth group at church about the trouble he had gotten into with the boys from school. It was hard for those in the group to believe that Paul, of all people, would be involved with something like that. Not just the fact that he was Pastor Joe's son, but they all looked up to him, because of his good character. They understood, however, how he could have been led astray, even though it was a brief interlude into the *world*. They were faced with it daily.

That is why Katherine felt she could make a difference by being a youth leader. To do that would be hard, because you had to be constantly aware of who you were. A child of the King.

There were others who looked to you when you were a youth minister, as their role model. Katherine had seen so many of her friends compromise themselves and their Christian beliefs due to the influence of others, who were not believers.

She was glad that even though Paul had slipped for two days, he had made the right choices and had done what he could to set things right. He would be able to identify with other kids when he ministered to them about their problems. This may have made him stronger in his convictions.

She had prayed that prayer for him the night he told the story to the group.

"Please, Lord. Let something good come out of the mess Paul nearly made in his life. Let him be convicted, in his heart that you were there all along, protecting him and guiding him to make the choices he knew to make.

"Please Lord; make him stronger in his walk with you, because of his experiences, so he can be an example to anyone else who may be tempted, as he was."

Paul had not known she prayed that prayer for him when she had gotten home from the meeting.

"Paul, I had a great time," said Katherine, as Paul walked her to her front door. "Thank you for the wonderful evening. I loved seeing the pictures of the glass chapel where your mom and Pastor Joe go for their annual vacation. It's such a beautiful place. And, your mom is good at taking photographs, isn't she? The food was out of this world, too. Everyone is right; your mother sure can cook."

Paul said, "Thanks, Katherine. You are right. Mom sure can cook. I like everything she makes, but her Cornish hens are one of my favorites. I guess that is why she made an extra one. After I shoot hoops tonight, I probably will finish that one off, too."

He reached out and took Katherine's hand and squeezed it lightly.

"Would you go bowling with me Friday night?" he asked. "I'm not that good a bowler, but I like to bowl."

"I would love to go with you. What time?" asked Katherine.

"Let's say seven. Would it be okay if Joey and Rachael go along? You know Rachel Smalley, she is in our youth group. If I have the car, then Joey is stuck at home."

"Oh, then, sure. That would be great!" exclaimed Katherine. "I just love Rachael. She has such a sweet spirit. And, Joey is so much fun. I have to warn you, though, that Rachel is a great bowler. She runs circles around me," Katherine laughed. "Being with them will be fun. We'll have a great time."

"She will probably run circles around me, too, but that's okay. Alright then, it's a date," said Paul. "Our *second* date," he added, laughingly.

The Power House

He let go of her hand and headed down the steps to the car, then, turned and waved and said, "Goodnight. Oh, and by the way, Katherine, you look *awesome* tonight."

He quickly got in the car, but he looked back as he drove away and saw her standing there with a big smile on her face, waving goodbye.

When he got home, Pastor Joe and Eva were still in the den with Joey, watching the ten o'clock news. Paul went in and leaned down to give his mother a hug.

"Thanks, Mom. I appreciate you and Dad letting me have Katherine over to dinner tonight. The dinner was really great. Katherine really liked the food."

"You are welcome, Paul. Katherine is a lovely girl. Your father and I have always admired her. We are just wondering why it took you so long to notice her," Eva laughed.

"It's got to be that it's God's timing, Mom, is all I say," said Paul, as he laughed along with his mother.

"I'm going to go shoot some hoops, Joey. Wanna go?" asked Paul.

"You betcha. Let me get the ball," said Joey, jumping up from in front of the television set.

As Paul started out the door, he said, "Oh, and Mom, you're right. *She is lovely.*"

Then he turned to run after his younger brother so she wouldn't see the big smile on his face, along with the flush coming up from his shirt collar.

CHAPTER SIXTEEN

Jessica Standish didn't sit with the other young people when she came to church on Sunday mornings. She always came to church alone. Her mother and father worked long hours at the local factory. Sunday was the only day they had to rest.

Jessica avoided going to Sunday school, although she was encouraged regularly by Mr. Thompson to join the rest of the youth in his Sunday School class that met before church. He would see her sitting near the back nearly every Sunday and would make a point of speaking to her and inviting her to his class.

Jessica was always polite, but never accepted his invitation to come to Sunday School.

One Sunday, Jessica was bending over to get her Bible and the notes she had taken from Pastor Joe's sermon. She felt someone tapping her on the shoulder. Startled, she turned to see Katherine West smiling at her. Jessica had always admired Katherine, although she was too timid to speak to her.

Katherine had a loving heart. She could sense that Jessica was shy, and that she seemed sad and lonely, always sitting in the back of the church by herself. She had tried

The Power House

several times to reach the back of the church before Jessica left, but so far, had been unsuccessful. Today, she was determined to talk to this lonely looking girl.

"I have been wanting to meet you," said Katherine. "I noticed you several Sunday's ago when I was leaving, but, somehow, you have been gone by the time I could get over to say hello. I feel like I have met you before, somewhere. My name is Katherine West," she said, extending her hand to Jessica.

"Hi," said Jessica, shyly. "It's nice to meet you."

She held out her hand to greet Katherine.

"Some of us from the youth group are having a picnic out by the lake. Would you like to come join us? There is plenty of food. All our mom's pack picnic baskets like they are expecting to feed King David's army," Katherine exclaimed with a laugh.

"Oh, no, thanks. I had better get home," said Jessica.

"Oh, Jessica, please come with us. It's such a beautiful day. There's going to be games, and singing. We are going to have lots of fun."

She could tell Jessica wanted to go, but, she was just too shy and needed some encouragement.

"Listen, you and I will sit together. I brought a big blanket and we can go down by the lake and talk, all by ourselves. I would like to get to know you," said Katherine with a smile.

"Well, alright," said Jessica. "If you are sure it's okay."

"Of course I am sure. Great, then come help me get the basket out of the car and we're off," said Katherine.

They spent the afternoon sitting by the lake. The grass had just been cut the day before, so there was a fresh smell of grass, along with soft breezes. It was a lovely day for a picnic. Katherine had been right. Her mother had packed enough food for King David's army.

Katherine and Jessica took what they wanted, then

shared the rest with some of the others in the group. They went back to the blanket to finish their conversation.

Jessica found that it was easy to talk to Katherine. She didn't ask probing questions about Jessica's family life like some people had. That was a subject Jessica didn't talk about freely. Some of the well meaning people in the church would ask her where her parents were. Why was she coming to church alone?

She avoided those people, moving to the other side of the church.

Jessica talked with Katherine about school, about the youth group and all the things they were doing. By the end of the afternoon, Jessica felt comfortable enough with Katherine to share something with her.

"You mentioned at the church that you felt you knew me from somewhere. I know where," she said.

"Really?" asked Katherine. "Because I know I have met you, but I apologize that I can't remember, for the life of me."

"It was at your house," said Jessica.

"At my house?" asked Katherine, pointing to her herself with a puzzled look on her face.

"Yes, last fall. My mother and father both work at the factory. They work at night and sleep during the day. So, basically I am home alone. I go to school all day, and when I get home, they have left for work. I am in bed by the time they come home from work."

"Since you know my parents work at the factory, you must know we don't have a lot of money. I work to help pay for school clothes, and all. I go door to door selling cosmetics. I don't do the home parties because, well, because, it's a little overwhelming for me. But, I don't mind showing people the products in their homes. That's where I met you," she said.

"That's right! I remember now," said Katherine. "I got that cute makeup bag from you when I ordered three

The Power House

lipsticks. But, you never came back by. Have you stopped selling?" she asked.

"No, I'm still selling," said Jessica.

She hung her head for a moment and then looked up at Katherine, with tears forming in her eyes.

"What's the matter, Jessica?" asked Katherine, reaching out to touch Jessica's hand.

"I'm sorry, I can't believe I am doing this again," said Jessica.

She turned her head and looked away, hoping the tears would stop.

"Katherine, the day I came by your house, it was raining. Mama and Daddy were both at work. They have to take the car to work. It's the only one we own. So, when I go out selling, I have to walk wherever I go. Anyhow, I went out to sell cosmetics, and it was in the fall, like I told you. I was so lonely that day. It was about dinner time and all the lights in people's houses had started coming on by the time I got out to work."

"I stopped outside your house, and I could see you sitting at a table, writing something. There was a fire going in the fireplace behind you and your mother was there with you."

"I just stood there in the rain for quite some time, just looking at that scene. It looked like something from a Norman Rockwell painting. I don't think I have ever felt as alone as I did at that moment," Jessica said, with a catch in her voice.

Jessica stopped and wiped her eyes.

"I was cold and wet, and I would have given anything to have had my mother at home in a warm kitchen fixing dinner, waiting on me to come home."

"I knocked and you came to the door. You were so nice to me. You invited me in. Your mother was taking some wonderful smelling something out of the oven right then, and she sat it down and came over to say hello."

The Power House

"You were both so kind. I remember you ordering the lipsticks, and your mother getting the bath products. It was my best order that week."

"The two of you were having so much fun together, picking out products. You seemed so close. Anyway, that's where you have seen me," she finished.

"Why, Jessica, Mother and I just love your products. She asked me the other day where we got those bath crystals. She wants to order some more," said Katherine.

"I was hurting so bad that day after I came by your house, I have avoided your street ever since. I guess I thought I would keep having the same feeling, if I stopped in again. Honestly, every time I see you at church, I have that image in my mind of you sitting there in the kitchen with your mom. You are very lucky, Katherine, do you know that?" said Jessica, looking up at Katherine.

"Jessica, I know that I am blessed to have a mom like mine. I am sorry you were lonely that day. I know it must be hard, with your parents working like that. I know they probably can't help being gone, but, it doesn't help that you are left all alone all the time. I can only imagine how you felt, standing out in the rain. The way you described it makes me almost feel as if I were out there with you, looking in. What you just described makes me realize, even more, how lucky I am. But, I prefer to call it blessed. I truly am blessed. But, I am so sorry that you had to feel that way," said Katherine.

"It's okay most of the time. I am used to it. It's just that day that sticks in my mind. It was like everyone in the world had a warm house and a happy family to be with, except me. Maybe it was a pity party, I don't know. But, I didn't feel envious of you, I just felt sad for myself that I didn't have anyone to go home to," said Jessica.

"Well, I think I know how we can fix some of that loneliness, even if we can't do anything about your parents work schedule," said Katherine.

"Let's start with a make up party. I know that the girls in youth group would love it. I could get everyone together about six o'clock one evening. That would give everyone time to go home and get their homework done. Then, we could all meet here at the church and have pizza. You can teach me your makeup tricks and I will help you do the presentation. How about that?" asked Katherine.

Jessica looked at Katherine and smiled.

"That would be wonderful!" she exclaimed. "Would you really want to do that?" she asked.

"Not only would *I* love to do it, I know most of the girls here would think it would be a *blast.* Let's do it. You need to meet everyone and this is a great way to start," said Katherine.

"Oh, and you know what else? My mom would probably like to have a makeup party, too. We have this family joke. She said her mother always used to use makeup, and some of her friends that didn't, teased her about it."

"She said that Grandma used to tell them, "*Well, the older the barn, the greater need for the paint.*" So now, when I am going upstairs to get ready for something, I tell Mom that I am going upstairs to paint my barn," Katherine laughed.

Jessica thought the story was hilarious. She laughed, as Katherine told about the barn painting.

"Then, if you are sure, let's plan on doing it. If you help me, I know we will have a great time," said Jessica.

"Listen, they are starting to sing praise songs. Let's go join them and I will introduce you to some of the girls right now," said Katherine.

Jessica and Katherine joined the others near the gazebo. Standing next to Katherine, Jessica sang with a strong, clear voice. Katherine noticed right away that Jessica had a beautiful singing voice.

"Oh, Jessica, your *voice.* You have a *lovely* voice. Why don't you come for choir practice on Wednesday night? We really need you in youth choir. You can do solos with a voice as strong as yours," said Katherine.

Jessica smiled.

"I would love to, Katherine," she replied.

Then, bravely, she mentioned that she wrote Christian songs, and played the piano. Katherine told her she couldn't wait to hear the songs and to hear Jessica play.

Two weeks later, Jessica and Katherine hosted a party for the girls in the youth group. At the end of the evening, Jessica had made many new friends. All of them invited her to come to the youth group meetings.

She finally felt like she belonged. The loneliness started to disappear after that evening.

Thus began what would become a life-long friendship between Katherine West and Jessica Standish.

Jessica blossomed under Katherine's love and attention. She made many friends from the youth group. When the choir director for the youth group heard Jessica sing, she immediately asked her to join the choir as a soloist.

Jessica became a member of the youth choir and began to attend most of the activities surrounding the group.

Her life was changed from being a lonely girl, with no friends and nowhere to go, to being active and outgoing, with many friends who loved her.

All because Katherine West took the time to reach out to a young girl sitting alone on Sundays in the back row of the church.

In doing this, Katherine showed she truly had a heart for God and a compassion for people. She was following the commandment of Jesus as found in John 15:12:

"This is my commandment, that you love one another as I have loved you."

Along with many other gifts of the spirit, God had given Katherine the gift of encouragement. She used it for His glory.

CHAPTER SEVENTEEN

After teaching a language class at seminary one day, Pastor Joe was on his way home when it began to rain heavily - an unexpected downpour.

He always took the same route from the seminary to his house, but, today he drove past his regular turn, going a few blocks out of his way. He did not know at the time why he did this. It seemed as though the Holy Spirit was guiding him through the rain soaked streets for a purpose. He had become sensitive to listening to the Holy Spirit years before. He always tried to follow what he was being led to do, even though he might not understand the reason at the time.

He reached to wipe the fog from the inside of his windshield.

Out of the corner of his eye, he saw a man, a woman and two small children sitting on the side of the road. In the man's hand was a crude sign, *"from out of town, broke down, please help us."*

The car in front of Joseph stopped, as the man inside leaned out to hand the man some change. As the man came to the car to take the money, people behind him started blowing their car horns, rolling down their windows, yelling at him to get out of the road.

The Power House

Joseph noticed the man hurry to the car, then turn. With an air of humility, he seemed to be trying to apologize to those honking their horns at him. There was something about him that made Joseph realize the family was truly in trouble, not panhandling on the street.

He turned the wheel, sharply, and pulled his car to the side of the road. The man had begun to run back to his family underneath the overpass.

Joseph got out of his car. He grabbed his umbrella from the back seat and walked through the rain to the family huddled underneath the overpass at the intersection.

The rain was so heavy, the covering did very little to protect them. The woman was trying to keep the small children, a boy and a girl, dry, but to little avail.

Joseph went to the man and said, "Hi, I am Pastor Joseph DuPriest. I teach a class in the evenings at the seminary around the corner. I was just on my way home. I see you are in need of some help. My car is over there," he said, pointing towards the road. "Bring your family and I will try to help you."

The man turned to his wife, and motioned for her to bring the children to the car. She quickly gathered her things and settled the children in the back seat of Pastor Joe's automobile.

Pastor Joe got into the driver's seat and closed the door to the pouring rain.

He turned to the man and said, "Let's get out of the way of traffic. Then we can talk."

The man nodded in agreement, so Pastor Joe pulled back into the traffic lane and headed down the street toward a convenience store.

He pulled into a parking space, turned off the engine and asked the man,

"What is your name?"

"Ramone Gonzales, sir. This is my wife Rosalita, and

my children Rudy and Martina. We are from Mexico. We came to the United States with a man who I thought was a friend. We came to see my mother who was in the hospital. She died three days ago," he said.

He paused for a moment, gazed out the window, and tried to begin again.

"This man, we found out, had other reasons for wanting us to ride to the United States with him. He was not a good man. After my mother died, he said he was not going back to Mexico. He said we needed to find another way to return home. He offered to take us to the bus terminal, so I agreed."

"When we got there, we all got out. He said for me to give him the money for our tickets and he would go and buy them, while my wife and I took the children to the bathroom, before we got on the bus. When we got back, he had left the terminal. We never saw him again," he concluded.

Pastor Joe said, "I am sorry to hear about all this. I truly am sorry about your mother, Ramone. This has to be very hard for you."

Ramone looked at Pastor Joe with tears beginning to well up in his eyes.

"Yes, sir, it is very, very hard," he said.

"Do you have any money at all?" Pastor Joe asked Ramone.

"Only a few dollars that I just now collected from people driving by on the highway. Sir, he took our luggage. My coat was in the car with my wallet in it. He took everything. The only thing we have is our visas. They were in Rosalita's handbag that she had with her. Unfortunately, I do not know anyone in the United States who could help us. My mother was the only one. She had been here for five years working as a housekeeper," he explained.

He rubbed his forehead with his hand, wiping away the raindrops. Then he continued.

"I asked the lady at the bus station what to do. She made

The Power House

this sign and told us to stand out by the road and try to get enough money for bus tickets. She was trying to be kind, but her boss came up and told us to move along. He told her that her job was to sell tickets, that she hadn't been hired as a charity worker. So, we went to the road and that is where we met you."

Pastor Joe looked in the back seat to find two small children with large sad eyes, looking directly at him. The woman kept her head down, as though she felt ashamed to be in this situation.

"I am going to help you, Rosalita. Don't worry about anything, okay?" said Pastor Joe, reassuringly.

The woman raised her head and looked at Pastor Joe.

With a heavy sigh, she said, "You are very kind, sir. My children are so wet from the rain, and they are very hungry. We were there for hours before you stopped to help us."

"First things first," said Pastor Joe. "I know a place where we can get dry clothes for all of you, and the best food in town. I am taking you home with me."

Ramone grabbed Pastor Joe's hand.

With a sob catching in his throat he said, "Oh, God bless you, sir. He will reward you for your kindness, though I can not do so myself. At least, not right now. The Lord has answered our prayers, Rosalita. Thank you, Dear Lord."

Pastor Joe brightened when he heard Ramone mention God and prayer. He knew, without a doubt, that God had guided him two blocks past his regular turn, and that this was what he was meant to do.

He also knew that *God had a greater reason for him to meet these people than just to help them at the present time.* He felt it in his spirit.

Pastor Joe pulled the car into his driveway, noticing that his wife, Eva, was already at home. He could see her in the kitchen window, waving to him as he stopped the car near the back door.

The Power House

It was still raining heavily, as he gathered his new friends and headed into the house. Eva met him at the door. He put his umbrella in the stand.

Pastor Joe hugged his wife and said, "Eva, this is Ramone Gonzales and his wife Rosalita. This is Rudy, and this is Martina. They ran into a bit of trouble on the road, and the Lord has sent them here for some dry clothes and a good dinner. I can tell from the smell, when I came in the door that they are in for a treat."

Eva smiled, greeted the couple, and took their dripping coats from them.

"Come on upstairs, Rosalita, and bring the children. Your little girl may have to wear some boy's jeans, but they will be dry. Our good friend, Anna, keeps some clothes over here for her son, David Joseph. I have some things you can wear, too," Eva said to Rosalita.

First, though, Eva stopped and gave each child a hug. Then, sensing that they were very hungry, she got them each a glass of milk to drink.

Eva and Rosalita took the children upstairs, where Eva began to gather clothing for them. Paul and Joey were at youth camp for the weekend, so there was plenty of room and privacy for their guests.

"The bathroom is right here. You should find everything you need. Go ahead and let the children take a hot bath. They look like they are really cold. There are towels under the sink. In the meantime, I will go down and finish dinner. We will take care of your wet clothing after dinner. Come on down when you are ready."

She stopped and gave Rosalita a hug and whispered to her, "Things are going to get better now. Don't worry about anything, okay? Everything is going to be alright. I will see you downstairs when you are ready to come down."

Thirty minutes later, a drier, and more composed, Rosalita came downstairs with Rudy and Martina. Eva had dinner ready at the large table in the kitchen. The children sat down, feeling instantly at ease in the warm, comfortable atmosphere of the kitchen of Pastor Joe and Eva DuPriest. They were very hungry, and eagerly eyed the roast beef with parsley potatoes, carrots and green beans that Eva had just placed before them on the table.

After returning thanks, Pastor Joe explained the situation to Eva, from the time he had left his class at the seminary, to finding Ramone and his family by the side of the road. The church had an emergency fund for such situations, so he already knew there was money available for getting the family back home to Mexico. First, though, he would like to hear more about Ramone and his family.

He just knew that God had a greater purpose in mind for him meeting these particular people.

After dinner, Pastor Joe invited Ramone to visit with him in the den, while Rosalita took the children upstairs to bed, and Eva did the dishes.

Ramone sat sipping his coffee by the fire. Pastor Joe asked him to tell him about himself and his family. They spent the next several hours talking about Mexico. They talked of Ramone and Rosalita's hometown, how they met, and how they came to know the Lord.

At the end of the evening, Pastor Joe felt he had made a life-long friend. He promised to get Ramone and his family on the bus back to Mexico the next day. Together, they prayed for a safe trip home. They thanked God for having sent Pastor Joe two streets past his regular turn on his way home. Together, they asked for God's will to be done in this *chance* meeting.

After Ramone, Rosalita, and their children were safely on the bus the next day, Eva and Pastor Joe had an opportunity to talk about the situation in which God had just used them.

Eva told her husband that she had thought about it the evening before, after everyone had gone to bed.

"There is a need for a homeless shelter here in our town," Eva said, emphatically, to her husband. "Why, Joe, I know at least a dozen of the ladies and their husbands who would be willing to volunteer time to open a homeless shelter."

She had already begun formulating plans in her mind. There would be a need for a building, for donations of furnishings, and they would need to put in a kitchen.

Pastor Joe agreed with Eva about the need for the shelter. He could sense her excitement, and he knew what organizational skills Eva had. Eva had a terrific idea, and Pastor Joe shared her enthusiasm.

Months later, out of that *chance* meeting in the rain with Ramone and Rosalita, came the grand opening of The Shepherd's Shelter. It was sponsored by *the church with no name* that met in the old high school auditorium. God had, once again, used a situation to turn evil into something good.

CHAPTER EIGHTEEN

Ramone Gonzales, his wife Rosalita, and their children arrived safely back home in Mexico. Ramone wasted no time in witnessing to people about the help God had provided his family while they were in America.

Most of the conversations heard outside the church were centered around a part of the population that did not embrace Americans.

The local people seemed always to speak badly about them. They envied what they themselves did not have. They did not know any Americans personally, but generation after generation told stories about the wealth they had heard was experienced by so many in America, while they labored daily for meager wages. Some people embellished their stories to the point of saying that all Americans were heartless and uncaring about people in foreign countries, people who had less than they had.

Ramone knew this to be untrue. He had never joined in those stories. He judged people only by what he saw in a person's character, not by their nationality, color, or their race.

At church that Sunday, Ramone felt the Holy Spirit urge him to testify before the congregation at his church. He was compelled to tell the story of how God provided in his family's hour of need.

A humble man by nature, Ramone felt empowered to stand before the church and tell the story of how a fellow Mexican citizen, a man whom he thought to be a friend, had betrayed him. He went on to tell how some Americans stopped in the rain to give him money.

He told how other people were angry and honked their car horns at him as he went to the car to receive the money, because he took time to say *thank you* to the giver.

Then, he told of Pastor Joe, and how God had him take a different route home that night, because God had children in need just around the corner. He told how Pastor Joe was used by God as an instrument in answering the prayers of Ramone and his wife Rosalita.

Ramone never tired of telling the story of how God rescued him in his time of distress, or of testifying for his love of Jesus and how he had been saved.

One particular Sunday, Ramone's pastor preached on the story of the Good Samaritan. At the beginning of the sermon, he asked Ramone to give his testimony of what had happened with him and his family in America, and how God used someone to help them.

Ramone eagerly accepted the invitation of the pastor to share, once again, the experience of the young pastor of the *church with no name* that rescued him and his family that rainy evening in America.

In the congregation that day sat Emmanuel Cortinez. Emmanuel was a very wealthy man. He owned nine refineries, some in Mexico, and some in South America. He did not attend this church regularly, but he came there when he was in the area on business. He came today to worship God, and to pray for strength in helping him to deal with the diagnosis he had just been given the past week.

Emmanuel was told he had cancer of the pancreas and

The Power House

had less than a year to live. He was an older man, in his late seventies. He had lived a full life and was not afraid to die.

He had not yet started feeling the ill effects of the disease on his body. In fact, he felt particularly good that day. He was in the area to talk with the manager of the local metal refining company, which he owned. He listened with interest to the story being told by Ramone Gonzales.

Emmanuel knew many Americans. He had always felt sad about the way a majority of his people viewed them, although he knew that many Americans actually felt superior to his people, as well.

The man, Pastor Joe, of whom Ramone spoke, sounded like a good man, and a true man of God. Emmanuel wanted to know more about him.

After the service, Emmanuel went to Ramone and said, "I am Emmanuel Cortinez. Please call me Emmanuel. I heard you speak, and I would like to talk more with you about Pastor Joe, and how he helped you and your family when you were in America. Will you and your family join me for lunch?"

Ramone looked at his wife, and she nodded her consent.

"We will go to my apartment, if that if alright with you. We will have whatever has been prepared for me," said Emmanuel.

Ramone did not know what that last statement meant. He thought, perhaps, that Emmanuel lived in one of the apartments nearby that housed the elderly. They had their meals prepared for them, as well as many of their other needs tended.

The place Ramone was thinking of was not very attractive from the outside, but he had heard the people were well cared for there. Therefore, he was very surprised when he and his family stepped outside the church with Emmanuel to find a black stretch limousine waiting to take them to lunch. The children's eyes were wide, and when Ramone

The Power House

looked at Rosalita, he saw that hers were, as well.

The driver took them to a beautiful *apartment*, as Emmanuel had called it. In America, it is known as a condominium. Emmanuel owned the entire complex, but kept the top floor for himself. He had an office there, as well as his own living quarters.

As they entered the apartment, they were greeted by a delightful aroma coming from the kitchen area. The table had been set with fine china, a linen tablecloth, silverware, and the candles on the table were already burning.

The home of Emmanuel Cortinez presented a warm and welcoming atmosphere.

Emmanuel's housekeeper, Carmen, came into the living room from the kitchen to greet Mr. Cortinez and his guests. She acted as though she was not surprised to see him with four other people, although he rarely brought people home on Sunday, after church.

There was plenty of food. She had prepared enough for a lunch the next day that Mr. Cortinez would be having before a meeting there in his office.

After they finished an exquisite lunch of Carmen's famous cooking, Emmanuel invited the children to go outside to the pool.

Carmen furnished them with bathing suits kept there for the businessmen and their families when they came to visit. It seemed as though she had a size to fit anyone, large or small.

The children were excited and could not wait to get into the water. Rosalita chose to sit beside the pool and watch them, so the men could talk.

"Ramone, please tell me your story, all over again, from the beginning. First though, I want to hear the name of this man who tricked you in America, and took all of your money and your belongings. Then, I want you to tell me everything about what happened to you from that point on.

And, especially about Pastor Joe and his *church with no name*," said Emmanuel.

They spent the next hour and a half talking about what had happened to Ramone in America.

Then, Emmanuel looked at Ramone and said, "Now I want you to tell me about yourself. What do you do for a living? Where do you live? How did you come to know the Lord?"

Ramone answered Emmanuel's questions to the best of his ability, beginning with the fact that he had worked for a manufacturing plant about twenty miles from the city for the past fifteen years. He was one of the managers, second only to the lead manager who had been there for twenty years.

After listening to Ramone's story, Emmanuel said, "I have an unusual request, Ramone. I would like for you to come tour my plant right outside the city. Come with me in the morning. Can you do that?" Emmanuel asked Ramone.

Ramone stared at Emmanuel for a moment, then, said, "Certainly, I would be happy to. I have a few days left before I have to report back to my job. But, why do you want me to do that, sir?"

"Because, if you like what you see, I would like to offer you the job of running the plant for me," said Emmanuel.

"The manager of this plant is being sent to my new plant in South America within the next month. That would give him time to teach you what he knows about the plant, and what you must know to manage it. If you have worked in another manufacturing plant for fifteen years, you already know most of what you need to know."

Seeing the surprise on Ramone's face at what he was hearing, Emmanuel explained, "Ramone, I know in my heart that you are a trustworthy man. A God-fearing man. I know you are skilled and knowledgeable. Ramone, the Lord wants me to give you this opportunity."

"Also, I would like you to attend the business meeting I

The Power House

am having after lunch tomorrow, if you are interested in the job," continued Emmanuel.

Ramone said, "I am honored by your faith in me. Truly honored. I will tour your plant, sir, but I must pray about the job part of it. I must consider what is good for my family and Rosalita and I must seek the guidance of the Lord before making a decision like that."

He seemed very surprised, but pleased, when Emmanuel said, "Let us go to the Lord together in prayer, this moment, and ask Him to guide you."

Each man reached out and clasped hands as though they were shaking hands in a greeting. They bowed their heads and began to pray. After they finished praying, Rosalita came towards them with an inquisitive look on her face, but smiling at Ramone and Emmanuel.

"Mr. Cortinez," she began.

"Emmanuel, please. Call me Emmanuel," he said to Rosalita.

"Yes, well, then. Emmanuel, I want to thank you so much for your hospitality today. The children seldom have a chance to swim. They had such a wonderful time. And Carmen's food was delicious. I wish I could cook like that myself. I am sure Ramone wishes the same thing," she said with a laugh.

"My pleasure. I am just sorry I didn't have the opportunity to visit more with you and the children. Maybe, if God is willing, there will be other opportunities," replied Emmanuel.

Ramone took that statement to mean *if he took the job*. That was true, but only in part. Emmanuel had not revealed anything about the news he had been given that very week, concerning his health, and that was what he was thinking, if God was willing to give him more time.

They said their goodbyes to Carmen. The limousine driver took them back to the church to get their automobile. After they had gone, Emmanuel went into his office and sat down at his desk. He made several telephone calls, and then went to lie down for the afternoon. He normally did not indulge in the traditional siesta, however, he had things to do, and could not afford to tire too easily before his work was finished.

Emmanuel and Ramone were both early risers. Emmanuel was downstairs in the lobby when Ramone arrived, so they got an early start out of the city to tour the metal refining plant. Ramone noticed right away that the plant was in excellent condition. The manager was obviously very good at his job.

Ramone decided that must be one reason for the manager being promoted to the newest and largest plant, the one in South America.

After spending several hours touring the plant, they went back to the apartment for lunch, and the business meeting that was to be held later in the afternoon. Ramone was now ready to give his answer to Emmanuel.

"I have prayed most of last night, Emmanuel," Ramone began. "I talked to Rosalita, and I put out a fleece before the Lord. The fleece was answered today when I met Eduardo, your plant manager."

Emmanuel looked at Ramone, waiting for him to continue.

"When I went into his office, you probably noticed me looking around," said Ramone.

Emmanuel nodded, indicating that he had seen Ramone looking around the manager's office.

"I saw what I was looking for. It was the answer to my fleece I put before the Lord, to show me if I should take the job you offered. A copy of the word of God, the Bible, there in plain sight on his desk," Ramone said, with a smile.

Emmanuel smiled, too. He had given that very Bible to Eduardo two years before, when he had asked Emmanuel about how to become a Christian. Not only had Eduardo become a Christian, he was such an example to the men who worked for him, some began seeking Christ on their own.

As a result, many lives had been led to the Lord. Maybe that was part of the reason there was such a sense of organization and camaraderie in the plant.

"I would like to work with you, sir, if you still want me there. I believe that is what the Lord would have me do," said Ramone.

Emmanuel smiled and said, "Of course I still want you. It is no coincidence, Ramone, that I was in your area on Sunday, and heard you speak in church. It is no coincidence that you have worked in manufacturing, and that I now need a good manager. These are just some of the plans God has that He has set in motion. I know He has others, and I am seeking Him about that right now."

"Other plans?" asked Ramone.

"You will know of the other plans later, son. Later," said Emmanuel as they looked up to greet the people coming for the meeting.

That night, Emmanuel received a telephone call that gave him the answers to some of the questions he had asked when he made his telephone calls the day before.

He called Carmen in and asked her to begin packing some of his clothes for a brief trip. He was about to leave early in the morning for America.

CHAPTER NINETEEN

His pilot, Jose Garcia, had the small jet ready when Emmanuel arrived at the airport at sunrise. Jose rushed out to greet Emmanuel, happy to see his longtime employer.

"I have already filed the flight plan. We have clearance, so I am ready to go when you are," said Jose.

He took Emmanuel's overnight bag, his briefcase, and his coat from him.

Emmanuel said, "I am ready. Let's fly."

In a few moments, they were taxiing down the runway and were airborne. It would take hours to fly to the United States, so Emmanuel leaned the soft leather seat back and slept.

The next thing he knew, Jose was shaking him and saying, "Mr. Cortinez, we have arrived in America."

Emmanuel could not believe how long he had slept. He felt refreshed. However, it did make him wonder if the illness the doctors had diagnosed was beginning to take its toll on his health.

He shook off the negative feeling, grabbed his briefcase and headed for the door of the plane. It took only a few moments, then, he was standing on American soil. The pilot told him his car was waiting for him, after he cleared Immigration.

Emmanuel went through Immigration and found his driver. He instructed the driver to take him downtown for a scheduled meeting in one of the main buildings.

When he arrived downtown, Emmanuel met with Milo Borzone, the investigator to whom he had made the telephone call the previous day.

Mr. Borzone assured him that Victorio Salinas had been arrested that morning and was sitting in jail at that very moment.

Victorio Salinas was the man who had stolen Ramone's money and his belongings. When he was arrested, the police had found Ramone's wallet, along with six others in the trunk of Victorio's car.

They also found a hidden compartment filled with illegal substances and guns, and discovered that he was in the country illegally.

Be sure your sins will find you out, thought Emmanuel.

He could not understand why Victorio had left Ramone's billfold in the trunk of his car after so long a time.

Mr. Borzone told him that, to someone like Victorio, it was like collecting trophies.

Emmanuel asked Mr. Borzone to have his secretary type a report about the arrest and have it sent immediately to the attention of Ramone Gonzales in Mexico.

He asked the secretary to write the words in the letter in quotes, "Evil pursues sinners, but to the righteous, good shall be repaid." *Proverbs 13:21.*

"Please sign the letter, "Your Brother in Christ Jesus. Emmanuel Cortinez," Emmanuel instructed the secretary.

"And, on that note, I am off to fulfill my *other* reason for coming to America," he said.

He called his driver to bring the car around. He gave him the street address of the old high school auditorium on the

The Power House

edge of the city, the building that housed the *church with no name*.

As Emmanuel's limo approached the church, he saw a man waving goodbye, as a bus pulled away from the building. The bus was loaded with young people from the church. They shouted and waved to the man, as he watched them leave.

The man stopped waving, then, looked around to see a limousine driving past the bus, turning into the driveway. As the car came to a stop, the driver rushed around the car to open the door for Emmanuel.

Emmanuel got out of the limousine and started towards the man, striding like a man with a purpose. The man walked forward to greet his visitor.

He reached Emmanuel, stretched out his hand and said, "Good afternoon. I am Pastor Joseph Dupriest. How can I help you?"

"Just the man I am looking for. Pastor Joe, I believe you are called," said Emmanuel, shaking Pastor Joe's outstretched hand.

"That's right," said Pastor Joe with a big smile.

"I am Emmanuel Cortinez and I just arrived from Mexico this morning. I am a friend of Ramone Gonzales. I came to personally thank you for what you did for him and his family when he was in America several months ago."

"Why, that's very kind of you. I appreciate your coming by to tell me that. Are you in the states on business?" asked Pastor Joe.

"If you don't mind, could we go inside and talk for awhile? I hope I am not interfering with your schedule. Maybe I should have called first for an appointment?"

"Not at all. Come on inside, and I will see if Anna has some coffee left from lunch," said Pastor Joe.

"That sounds wonderful," said Emmanuel.

Pastor Joe opened the door for him and they went into the office that was Pastor Joe's study.

The Power House

"Please sit down, Mr. Cortinez."

"You asked me a question, as we were standing outside. I would like to answer that question now. Yes, I am in the states on business. My business is with you," said Emmanuel.

Pastor Joe looked puzzled.

"I am sorry, I don't understand."

"Let me start at the beginning," began Emmanuel.

"I have a branch of my company near the city where Ramone and his family live. When I am at the branch, I attend the same church Ramone and his family attend."

"The Sunday I was there last, Ramone gave his testimony about how the Lord had used you to help him in the situation that occurred when he came to see his mother. By the way, the authorities have arrested the man who did this terrible thing to Ramone and Rosalita and their children," he added.

"That is good news," said Pastor Joe. "Were you instrumental in that arrest?"

"I will just say there is an advantage to having connections," said Emmanuel. "But, that is not what I came here today to talk to you about. I want to talk about your church."

"Certainly," said Pastor Joe. "God has blessed us so much since Eva and I began this ministry. I wanted to tell the story of Jesus Christ, to preach from the word of God. Our prayer was that He send those who needed to hear and be saved. We began with about twenty-five members who attended regularly, and last Sunday we recorded seven hundred eighty- eight in Sunday school, and twelve hundred and fifty in the Sunday service."

He paused, and shook his head.

"Sometimes I can hardly believe it when I hear those numbers. I guess it's because I don't know where we put them," he laughed.

"May I see the auditorium for myself?" asked Emmanuel.

"Certainly, sir. It's out the door here and down the hall. Come with me, I will show you," said Pastor Joe.

They started through the door as Anna was coming down the hallway.

"Anna, I would like you to meet Emmanuel Cortinez. He is from Mexico, a friend of Ramone and Rosalita Gonzales," said Pastor Joe, introducing Emmanuel to Anna.

"It is nice to meet you," said Anna, shaking hands with Emmanuel. "How are they? We haven't talked with them in a month or so."

"Oh, they are just fine, just fine. I will tell them you asked about them," Emmanuel replied.

"Could I get you something to drink?" asked Anna.

"Coffee would be nice, if you have it already made. I drink it black," said Emmanuel.

"Make that two, Anna, and thank you," Pastor Joe added.

"Two black coffees coming up," replied Anna. "I will bring them in when I see you come back."

Pastor Joe and Emmanuel went down the hallway and entered the auditorium.

It was like most old high school auditoriums, a stage up front with heavy maroon curtains. A podium had been placed in the center, made of clear heavy acrylic. The seats in the auditorium were padded folding chairs. They were packed in like sardines. Emmanuel walked over and sat in a chair, looking up at the stage.

"Very nice," he said.

"The Lord has been good," said Pastor Joe. "We have a giving congregation, but we all felt we should use our offerings to sponsor missions, rather than build a new church. And, we now also use some of the offerings to run our homeless shelter, the Shepherd's Shelter. By the way, did Ramone tell you the story of how that idea began?" he asked Emmanuel.

"Oh, yes, he mentioned it as a result of the way God turns evil to good," Emmanuel responded with a smile.

Pastor Joe smiled broadly.

"Sounds like he filled you in on quite a bit. Well, I am glad, because it has been a good thing for so many, including the people who work there. I work a regular schedule of two afternoons a week, and whenever they need someone to fill in. It is such a blessing. I do find myself ministering sometimes, rather than dishing up mashed potatoes," he laughed. "We have had so many souls won for Christ's kingdom. It's lots easier to listen when you have your stomach full."

"Praise the Lord Almighty for mashed potatoes," said Emmanuel, as he laughed along with Pastor Joe.

"Let's go have that coffee now," said Pastor Joe.

They went back to the pastor's study.

Pastor Joe sipped his coffee and waited for Emmanuel to speak. He was very curious as to why Emmanuel Cortinez would come to America to visit him.

"I mentioned before that I have a company. I own a metal refining company and have branches in Mexico and South America," said Emmanuel.

"God has blessed me. I had a wonderful wife for fifty three of my seventy eight years. Her name was Corina. She died three years ago."

"I am sorry to hear about your wife," said Pastor Joe.

"We had no children. She could not bear children, and she always grieved over that," Emmanuel mused. He paused, thinking of his wife, Corina.

"To make the story short, Pastor Joe, I have been told by my doctors I have only a year, at the most, to live. They say I have pancreatic cancer," Emmanuel stated frankly.

Pastor Joe leaned forward in his chair.

"Oh, no," he said. "Mr. Cortinez, I am sorry to hear that. Have you gotten a second opinion?"

"No, I just found out last week," said Emmanuel. "To tell you the truth, I just accepted the fact, and I have never thought of a second opinion. But, let me continue. I told you that to tell you this."

Emmanuel paused to take a deep breath before continuing.

"I had a dream the night before I heard the testimony given by Ramone. The Lord showed me a church, a beautiful church built on the side of a big lake. It had a large sanctuary that would house many people. The pews were made of mahogany. The church had a prayer room. There was a chapel that looked out over the lake. In the middle of the lake was a huge fountain, shaped like a cross. On each point of the cross where Jesus was nailed, water flowed from the fountain. There were small jets shooting water up around the cross. There was a stained glass window in the front of the church. The window had a figure of Jesus, surrounded by cut crystal glass that shone around Him like rays from his body. It was the most beautiful thing I have ever seen."

He stopped and wiped tears from his eyes.

"I looked for the sign at the front of the church. There was none. I saw a man walking by, and I asked the man what was the name of the church. He smiled at me and said, "It will be given to him." Then, he vanished into thin air. You see, Pastor Joe, *it was a church with no name!"* he exclaimed.

Pastor Joe was now sitting on the very edge of his chair. He could barely breathe. He waited for Emmanuel to continue.

"The next day, I attended church and heard Ramone speak. He told of his trip to America, his being robbed and left destitute. He told of Pastor Joe and Eva. And he told of *the church with no name."*

He paused for a moment, and the room became so quiet, you could have heard a pin drop. Then, Emmanuel spoke softly.

"Pastor Joe, I know that the Lord wants me to build that church for you. That's why he gave me the dream. That's the reason I saw the man who told me the church would be given a name. That's the reason he had me at that plant, so I would hear Ramone speak that day in church. And, I believe He meant that He will give *you* the name. You must listen for the word of the Lord in this, Pastor Joe."

Pastor Joe sat very still and said nothing. To say he was astounded was putting it mildly. As Emmanuel had talked, he envisioned what the church looked like, as he described it to him. His vision of it was beautiful. He could just imagine what Emmanuel had seen in his dream.

"The first thing I would like to know is, will you accept this as a gift from God, not from Emmanuel Cortinez. Because, we know that it says in James 1:17, *"Every good gift and every perfect gift is from above, and comes down from the Father of lights, with whom there is no variation or shadow of turning."*

"I would like you to present God's gift before your church next Sunday. If the doctors are right, I do not have much time. Pastor Joe, I pray that you *believe* that God gave me that dream the night before I heard Ramone speak, and that he showed me this church that he wants me to build to replace *the church with no name*. That is *your* church, Pastor Joe," said Emmanuel.

"But, before you present the gift to your congregation, I would like to ask you to pray that God will give you the name He has chosen for His church. If you will accept this gift, I will have a meeting this afternoon with an architect to do an artists' rendition of the church the Lord showed me. You can show that to your people on Sunday, as well," Emmanuel concluded.

Pastor Joe leaned back in his chair. He thought back on the night he had left the language class he had been teaching at the seminary. He thought of how the Holy Spirit led him to take a different route home that rainy evening. Of how he saw Ramone and Rosalita by the side of the road, soaked from the rain, and begging for money to get back home. He remembered the word he had from God when he finished talking later that evening with Ramone in the den.

"*God has a greater reason for you helping these people than just meeting their needs this evening.*"

All this time, he thought the reason was the Shepherd's Shelter. God had just revealed *His greater reason*, spoken in the words of Emmanuel Cortinez.

Pastor Joe sat for a moment.

Then he said softly, "Now, allow me tell you, as a dear fellow American, says, "*The rest of the story.*"

He told Emmanuel of what happened that night, months earlier, from his own perspective, and the words the Holy Spirit had spoken to him about how this was not a *chance* encounter.

There was to be a *greater purpose* for meeting Ramone and Rosalita Gonzales.

"I *do* believe God gave you that dream, Mr. Cortinez. I know that you were in church to hear that very testimony," said Pastor Joe.

At that point, his emotions overcame him, and Pastor Joe began to weep as he spoke.

"I have no choice about whether to accept your gift or not. I know, without a doubt, it is a gift from God. Excuse me, but this is truly overwhelming. Please forgive me for my tears. They are tears of both joy and amazement at how the Lord works in His mysterious ways," he said apologetically to Emmanuel.

"No apology necessary," said Emmanuel, wiping away tears of his own.

Pastor Joe came around the desk and embraced Emmanuel. They stood like that for a few moments, caught up in the joy of the Lord.

Finally, Emmanuel laughed softly and said, "Now, if you will excuse me, I have to go to a meeting with an architect."

Pastor Joe laughed a little. "God bless you, Mr. Cortinez,

that's all I can say. God bless you!"

"You must call me Emmanuel."

Pastor Joe's voice caught in a sob as he said, "*Emmanuel, God With Us*." That is what your name means. What an awesome significance that has for me."

He stood for a few moments, wiping away more tears, until he regained his composure.

Then, taking Emmanuel's hand he said, "Please, on bended knees. I want to pray to God, right now, for your healing. If God has chosen to use you in such a mighty and wonderful way, then I know He loves you as a chosen one of His children. I want to pray that He heals you completely. Will you stay for a moment, Emmanuel, and let me pray for you?"

"Certainly, Pastor Joe, I would be honored to have you pray for me."

Pastor Joe went to the corner curio and came back with a small wooden bottle.

"This is olive oil, Emmanuel. I want to anoint you with the oil and pray for you."

"Then, let it be done as you say," said Emmanuel.

There, in the make-shift study in the old high school auditorium, Pastor Joe knelt beside Emmanuel, put oil on his head and prayed for his healing.

"My Dear and Gracious Heavenly Father, I come to you on bended knees. I humbly acknowledge that you are Lord, Creator of all things. You have given me so many gifts, my dear Father. You tell us to eagerly desire the greater gift. Father, you have brought this man to me today. You have orchestrated in your Divine Plan for us to be here at this very moment. I desire the gift of healing, Father, to help my brother Emmanuel. I ask, Lord, that the reports he received from his physician be false. That You, the Great Physician, heal him. I pray that the cancer he was told he had be gone, in Your name. I thank you for his willingness to listen to

The Power House

your Spirit and that he is willing to obey you. Help me Father, to listen. To be sensitive to you, that I may know your will in naming this church. Help Emmanuel, by healing him, so he can be a part of it. I ask these things in the name of Jesus Christ, our Lord and Savior. Amen."

Emmanuel Cortinez stepped outside, looked up at the sky, and gave praise and glory to God. He felt wonderful. He felt as though he was floating on air. This dream was about to become a reality. He knew God would lead him to an artist that could do credit to the beauty of the vision of the church he had in his dream. He couldn't wait to see it on paper. He was about to set the wheels in motion.

He signaled for the driver to drive on, waving goodbye to Pastor Joe, with a promise to see him the next day. The driver stopped outside a twenty-four story building in the downtown section of the city. Emmanuel Cortinez took the elevator to the twenty second floor for his meeting with the architect.

Within two hours, the architect had produced a sketch of the church as Emmanuel described it to him. He asked Emmanuel to go with him to another department. When they stepped in the room, Emmanuel saw a vast array of equipment.

"Let me show you what this one does," said George Green, the head of the art department.

He showed Emmanuel how a computer image could be done from the sketch that had been made. Emmanuel could not believe what the computers were able to do. This was going to be much better than he had expected. Mr. Green assured him he would rush the project to be ready by Saturday, and have it delivered to Mr. Cortinez at his hotel. Emmanuel left the building, confident that he had chosen the right firm for the job.

CHAPTER TWENTY

It was early in the evening. Pastor Joe told Eva he needed to go to the church so he could be alone. He had told her about the meeting he had that afternoon with Emmanuel Cortinez. He asked her to not mention the meeting to anyone, or what Emmanuel had offered to do.

He also asked her to be praying that he be given a revelation from the Lord about the name for the beautiful new church that was about to be built. She hugged him as he went out the door.

"Just remember what Emmanuel said about the man in his dream. The man outside the church. Remember, he said, "*He* will be given the name. Emmanuel feels that you are the one to whom God will reveal the name. I believe it, too," said Eva.

Pastor Joe went to the car and started to the church. When he arrived at the building, *the church with no name*, he went inside the sanctuary and knelt at the altar. He intended to stay there until the name was revealed to him.

He stayed at the altar praying, then, grew quiet and waited for a word from the Lord.

Pastor Joe had always been an avid reader. He loved the works of C.S. Lewis, the poetry and songs of Fanny Crosby.

Most of all he loved the writings of Andrew Murray.

As he prayed at the altar that day, he was reminded of some of the words he had read over and over, written by Andrew Murray about the Holy Spirit. Mr. Murray had written in these words Pastor Joe recalled.

"Our prayer that our lives fulfill God's purpose must have its origin in God himself, the highest source of power."

As Pastor Joe thought about these words talking of God's purpose and of God Himself, the *Highest Source of Power*, he recalled the scripture from Luke 24:49.

"Behold I send the promise of my Father upon you, but tarry in the city of Jerusalem until you are endued with power from on high."

Remembering this scripture, Pastor Joe spoke the words out loud.

As he uttered the words, other words came to him in his spirit, *"There is power in the house of the Lord. The Great I Am is the Highest Source of Power."*

Pastor Joe smiled when he spoke those words.

"There is Power in the House of the Lord. He truly is the Highest Source of Power. Therefore, the church is a Power House."

He had his answer. He stretched himself out on the altar and face down on the carpet, kept himself still before the Lord, for over an hour.

He had been gone for several hours when Eva saw the headlights from his car pulling into the driveway.

She sat where she was and waited for him to come in, knowing he would come directly to her to tell her what God had revealed to him.

She looked up from her sewing as he came through the door to the den.

He had a smile on his face that told her everything. He had been given the name of the church that God had given them.

The Power House

His exuberant spirit was catching and Eva jumped up and ran to where he was standing. He told her of how he had prayed and asked God to reveal what he wanted him to know. As he talked of how God had led him to the name through His word, he began to lift his hands toward heaven.

"Oh, Eva, do you see all that has happened, all that God has provided from that one evening in our lives when He had me find Ramone? He knew that very night when I stopped to help Ramone that the Power House was coming into being from that action," he exclaimed. "I know there are so many things He has done in my life that I only found out the reasons for later, but this is the one to top them all."

"Eva, come here," said Pastor Joe, reaching for his wife.

Eva came to him. He put his arms around her and said, "Let's thank the Lord together for what he has done."

Eva took his hand and they knelt beside the fireplace, praising God and thanking Him for his goodness, grace, and provision.

On Saturday afternoon, Emmanuel Cortinez called Pastor Joe and asked if he would come by the hotel to pick up the picture that had been done of the proposed church. Pastor Joe asked if it was alright to bring Eva.

Emmanuel replied, "By all means. I would love to meet her. She should be part of this."

When Pastor Joe and Eva arrived at the hotel, they were greeted at the door of his suite by Emmanuel himself.

After the introductions were made, Emmanuel said, "Come, come. I cannot wait for you to see this."

He stepped over to the window where an easel stood. He pulled the cover from the frame holding the picture. Pastor Joe and Eva could only stand and stare.

It was more of a computer generated likeness than the painting they expected. The computer generation made the likeness of the church seem even more real. It showed a huge building. The lake was on the right side of the church, willow trees surrounding it.

The front of the building had a stained glass window with cut crystal glass all around the figure of Jesus. Jesus was depicted with arms outstretched as though calling for those who would to come to Him. The cut crystal glass emitted sharp rays of light that appeared to be coming from around the body of Christ. The effect was incredible.

Then they looked at the lake where the fountain, that was a large cross, flowed in the middle of the lake. Just as Emmanuel had described, the water was flowing from points where Jesus would have been nailed to the cross. There were jets shooting water up all around the cross.

There was no need for words. The tears and wide eyes of both Pastor Joe and Eva said it all.

"This is very close to what the Lord showed me in my dream," said Emmanuel. "I never imagined they could do such a wonderful job of capturing the vision of the church I saw that night."

He turned to Pastor Joe with an inquisitive look on his face.

"Now, Pastor Joe, I want to know. Has the Lord revealed the name of the church to you?" he asked.

Pastor Joe told Emmanuel of how his prayers had guided him to the name of *The Power House. A house of God filled with the Holy Spirit.*

"A perfect name from a perfect God," said Emmanuel.

"I would like to start building the church right away. The architect I am working with has had a realtor looking for the property and he believes he has found it. We will go together right now to look at it, if that is possible for you to do," he said to Pastor Joe and Eva.

Eva could not take her eyes off the picture. She had studied photography in college. She loved art, but had never seen anything quite as lovely as this picture done by the architectural firm.

"Of course, that would be wonderful. I know that if this is the property God has chosen for the church to be built on, He will confirm it in us," said Pastor Joe.

He squeezed Eva's hand.

He then said, "Emmanuel, thank you so much. I know that sounds lame, given the magnitude of what you are doing. But, thank you."

Emmanuel said, "You are welcome. But, please, from this point, no more thanks are necessary for Emmanuel Cortinez. The praise will be directed to God. Is that agreed?"

"Yes, I understand. Praise be to God. But, for Emmanuel Cortinez, as well as for the church," laughed Pastor Joe.

Emmanuel laughed, as did Eva. Then they gathered their things to go look at the property.

This was not a small lake the realtor was showing them. It covered eighty acres. The land surrounding the lake was part of the property, but the largest amount was on the left side of the lake.

It was beautiful and serene, with tall trees covering the property. All totaled, the land came to one hundred sixty acres, including the lake.

It would cost a fortune, but Emmanuel had a fortune that had been given him by God. A fortune predestined to include this transaction. He had been blessed. And now he was able to do the blessing he was called to do.

Pastor Joe and Emmanuel looked at each other after having spent twenty minutes on the property.

"Yes," they said in unison.

Eva nodded her head in agreement, full of the wonder of all that was happening.

The answer they gave made the architect and the realtor extremely happy as well. There were smiles shared that day among all who were present, but for different reasons for them all. The smiles from the architect and realtor were obviously from their anticipated financial gain.

The Power House

The smile from Emmanuel came from the joy of being able to do God's will. It involved the realization of the dream God had given him the night before he heard Ramone's story.

The smile from Pastor Joe was from the glory that God would be given for the gift and the souls who would be saved in this Power House.

The smile from Eva was from seeing how happy Pastor Joe was, and from knowing God's will was being done in such a miraculous way.

What a day of rejoicing that was for all those who stood on the property by the lake.

"And just think of what a story we have to tell the congregation tomorrow. You will be there, won't you Emmanuel?" asked Pastor Joe.

"Yes, I would love to be there, Pastor Joe. It will be a wonderful day."

And it *was* a wonderful day. The congregation was instructed to be patient and quiet from the beginning of the story Pastor Joe was going to tell them to the very end. No one was to speak or whisper amongst themselves.

Because of these instructions, they were all able to hear every word he spoke. They were aware that the Shepherd's Shelter had come about from the night Pastor Joe met Ramone Gonzales.

But, as Pastor Joe had so aptly put it to Emmanuel, this was *the rest of the story*.

Pastor Joe told the story of how Emmanuel had been in the church that morning when Ramone gave his testimony about meeting Pastor Joe and Eva. He told of the dream Emmanuel had the night before.

At the end of the story, he turned the easel around so that the work the architect had done was fully displayed to the congregation.

"So, brothers and sisters, we are soon to become

The Power House

members of what God has shown us. I present you with *The Power House*. We will no longer be known as *the church with no name*."

As he finished speaking, he said, "Now you may speak or make comments."

The silence was deafening for a few moments. Each member was thinking about the miraculous story they had just heard. They were staring at the beautiful characterization of the church.

Then, almost as a body, the congregation rose and began praising the Lord, clapping and cheering, thanking God for his gracious gift.

CHAPTER TWENTY ONE

Nine months later, construction on The Power House was completed. There was to be a building dedication before church services the next morning.

Pastor Joe was asked by the building committee to come to a meeting that afternoon, to go over the last minute details of the program for the next day.

When he entered the room, he quickly detected an air of excitement from the members in the meeting.

This will be a glorious day for the Lord. We are all very excited, he thought.

He took a seat at the side of the table and waited for Robert Ewing, the chairman of the committee, to start the meeting. All at once, he heard noises outside in the hallway.

Anna, Eva, Paul, and Joey came into the room and waved at Pastor Joe as they took a seat at the other end of the long conference table.

Everyone in the room looked at Pastor Joe, then, looked expectantly back at the door.

Pastor Joe glanced up and saw Emmanuel Cortinez as he entered the room with Ramone and Rosalita Gonzales on either side of him.

Pastor Joe practically shouted, as he jumped up to run

The Power House

to them.

"Emmanuel! Ramone! Rosalita! It has been so long since I've seen you. I can't *believe* you are all here. I thought you weren't going to be able to come for the dedication."

He went to Emmanuel first, and threw his arms around the older man. Emmanuel returned the affection for his good friend. Then, Pastor Joe turned and hugged Ramone and Rosalita.

"Before we continue with our meeting here this afternoon, Mr. Cortinez has something to share with you, Pastor Joe," said Robert.

Emmanuel went to the table and sat down beside Pastor Joe. Everyone in the room grew very quiet. Ramone and Rosalita took the chairs they were offered by Robert, and waited for Emmanuel to speak.

"Pastor Joe, I have some news that I wants to share personally with you. I took your advice. I went to M.D. Anderson Hospital in Texas and I got that second opinion you told me about. They did the same tests they did on me in Mexico. Pastor Joe, *they did not find any pancreatic cancer*. They found nothing wrong with me but old age!" said Emmanuel with a chuckle.

"Please let me say that the medical facility I went to in Mexico is a wonderful hospital with all the finest equipment and physicians. There is no doubt about it. Pastor Joe, the Lord healed me," he said loudly.

Then, in a soft whisper, "The Lord healed me," as though he still could not believe it himself.

Pastor Joe recalled the night when he anointed Emmanuel with oil and prayed that God give him healing. He had *believed* when he prayed the prayer that God was the Great Physician and that if it was His will, Emmanuel was healed.

"Oh my God, my gracious heavenly God!" cried Pastor Joe.

The Power House

Once again, as he had been doing throughout this entire adventure with Emmanuel, he wept.

Tears of joy, tears of gratitude, fell down his cheeks and he made no effort to restrain them. He never took his eyes off Emmanuel, so he did not see that there was not a dry eye in the room.

"I just thought I knew *the rest of the story*," laughed Pastor Joe, as he choked back a sob.

Robert Ewing cleared his throat and wiped his eyes with his handkerchief.

"Well, you really don't know all of it, yet, Pastor Joe."

"Ok, Robert, then let's have it."

Robert nodded to Emmanuel, who held a rolled up paper in his hands. He stepped up to the table and unrolled the paper.

He motioned for Pastor Joe and Eva to come stand beside him.

Pastor Joe moved to Emmanuel's side. He looked down at the papers, and saw that it was a blueprint. He looked questioningly at Emmanuel.

"A manse, Pastor Joe. A house for you and Eva, right on the lake down from the church. Plenty of room, see?"

Pastor Joe stood looking at Emmanuel, literally with his mouth hanging open.

"A house? A house for us? Oh, Emmanuel, this is too much," he said.

"A gift, Pastor Joe, partly from your congregation, partly from me."

Robert Ewing stepped forward, placing his hand on Pastor Joe's shoulder.

"You and Eva have served the church selflessly for many years now. You have only accepted two increases in salary over all these years."

"Every bit of money taken into the church up until this point has gone towards missions, or the shelter. This is a unified decision, Pastor Joe, from your congregation. We voted weeks ago, and it was a unanimous vote, to help build this home for you and Eva," said Robert. "Mr. Cortinez was generous enough to ask to contribute, as well."

"I am in shock. I just don't know what to say," said Pastor Joe, looking from Robert to Emmanuel.

"There is no need to say anything. Be gracious and accept this, Pastor Joe. Just be gracious," laughed Emmanuel.

Eva came to stand beside Pastor Joe.

"You already knew?" he asked his wife.

"Yes, dear, but they made me promise not to say anything. I was involved in all the planning. And, look at this, Joe."

She pointed to the blueprint.

"Your own private rose garden," she said, indicating a space on the plans. "Emmanuel wanted to be here for the surprise. Isn't it wonderful?" she exclaimed.

"I just don't know how to respond to all these blessings, at one time," said Pastor Joe.

"Graciously, Joe, graciously," laughed his wife.

When they got home that evening, Pastor Joe turned to Eva, giving her a hug.

"Eva, this has been the most incredible experience of my entire life. From the day I met Ramone and Rosalita, things have happened that I never would have dreamed could happen."

"And, now, this. Eva, you are finally going to have a beautiful new home. I know you love this one, but I can see your excitement over the new one, too. I am thrilled, but like I said, I am almost in shock at the generosity of the church, and of Emmanuel, in making this happen."

"Joe, I was just like you were when they first mentioned the idea to me. It took me almost a week to adjust to the idea of what they were doing. But, I see it as a gift of love, and I know they feel it is a way to thank you for all the time you have spent shepherding them, praying for them, helping

The Power House

them, during these past years.

I finally saw that it was their way of honoring you for your love and devotion."

"A new home, though, Eva. After we just finished building The Power House."

"The Power House," he repeated. "I remember less than a year ago when the Lord gave me the name for the new church. You know something, Eva? I have since come to realize that we have been in a *Power House* all along. Even when we were in the community room all those years ago. It, too, was a *Power House* for the Lord. A house filled with the Holy Spirit. Every church is a Power House. Or, at least, it should be."

"You are so right, Joe. I never thought of it that way, but you are so right," said Eva. "God has truly blessed *us* in enabling us to do the blessing of others for so many years."

"Eva, tomorrow will be a wonderful day. The day we dedicate The Power House to the Lord. Such a beautiful building. Oh, and Eva, just think of all the *seats* it has!" he laughed, as he picked her up and whirled her around the kitchen, as she laughed along with him.

CHAPTER TWENTY TWO

The Sunday night after Paul and Katherine both graduated from college, there was to be a celebration for the college graduates who attended the church. Everyone from the congregation was invited to attend.

Paul and Katherine had continued to see each other throughout their college years. They sat together in church, and worked together with the youth group on Sunday evenings. They were a couple of young people dedicated to doing the work of the Lord, and they were dedicated to one another.

That night, Eva went to the altar during the end of the service and knelt, thanking God for the call on Paul's life. She praised Him for giving Paul a scholarship to go to college. He had worked hard for it, but she always remembered to give credit to the Lord.

She thanked him for the call on Katherine's life as well. She knew the past year had been very difficult for Katherine, because she had lost her father to cancer. The graduation had a note of sadness in it, due to the fact that he wasn't there with the rest of Katherine's family to honor his daughter's graduation.

The ceremony began with Katherine walking down one

aisle, with the young women, and Paul coming down the other, with the young men. Pastor Joe and the elders of the church were waiting to greet them at the front, with gifts for all of them, and loving words of praise for their accomplishments.

After the speeches were made and they had received their gifts, Pastor Joe told the congregation that Paul and Katherine had an announcement of their own. They were engaged to be married. They had counseled with Pastor Joe and Eva a week before they graduated, so they knew what was to be announced after the ceremony that night. So did Katherine's family.

Paul had asked Katherine's mother for Katherine's hand in marriage two weeks before, and she gladly accepted him as her new son-in-law.

The congregation was not surprised, but they were extremely pleased that the young couple were going to become man and wife. It was a joyous day in the Power House.

The wedding was six months after the announcement.

Paul stood at the front of the church with Joey, his best man. He was waiting for his beautiful bride to stand with him, in front of his father, who was to marry them.

As the music started, he wiped his eyes as he thought of how proud Katherine's father would have been to walk her down the aisle today.

Jessica Standish, Katherine's maid of honor, walked down the aisle. Next came eight of Katherine's best friends. They all wore sky blue dresses, as soft as clouds. They were followed by twin girls who tossed rose petals in the aisle, as they came toward the altar.

Katherine came down the aisle on the arm of her mother. Rather than prelude music to the traditional wedding march, there was the music to, "*Where Are you Going, My Little One, Little One.*" There was not a dry eye in the house, as

The Power House

everyone thought of Mr. West and how much he had loved his daughter. He would have been so proud of her this day. The song was a reminder of the brevity of life itself.

"*Where are you going, my little one, little one? Where are you going, my baby, my own? Turn around you're tiny, turn around, you're grown, turn around you're a young wife with babes of your own,*" played softly, as Katherine and her mother walked slowly down the aisle.

Paul looked at his radiant bride. He remembered the night he picked her up for their first date. She wore white that night, too, with a blue satin ribbon in her long blonde hair. Today, she wore a simple, but elegant wedding gown. There were sky blue ribbons in her hair that was put up underneath the veil. He could feel his heart beginning to beat faster. She looked incredibly beautiful.

As Katherine and her mother reached the halfway mark up the aisle, the music changed to the traditional wedding march. The congregation rose, to watch Katherine West walk the rest of the way down the aisle to become Mrs. Paul DuPriest.

The vows were solemn, and carefully read and repeated, between Paul and Katherine. She felt that she must be the happiest girl in the entire world that day. She had liked Paul since she was fifteen years old, but it had taken him three more years to notice her.

They had dated for the past five years. It seemed like yesterday she had been in his home having dinner with his family for the first time. The years had passed so quickly.

She repeated her vows, slowly, and reverently, to Paul.

This promise to love and cherish is to Paul, but these vows in this marriage are really being made to you, Lord," thought Katherine.

My husband. Paul is really my husband, she thought.

It was a like a dream, but one she had been dreaming, for a long time.

The Power House

After the wedding, Paul and Katherine left on their honeymoon. They were going for two weeks to spend time in the mountains. They had a hotel already booked, compliments of Pastor Joe and Eva.

The hotel was old and quaint, with marble staircases and mahogany railings. There was a huge balcony that looked out over the mountainside. The balcony had white wicker chairs where people sat enjoying fresh lemonade and the view. Standing on the balcony, they could see the statue of Christ, standing with arms outstretched, seeming to preside over the entire area with His love and protection. It was truly a magnificent sight.

It was the same sight Pastor Joe and Eva experienced on their first trip there, years before.

Paul and Katherine DuPriest stood at the private balcony railing of the Bridal Suite. They were watching the sun set in the west. It was their first day of being man and wife, and they were very happy.

"It was so thoughtful of your parents to give us this trip as a wedding gift," said Katherine. "Oh, Paul, I am so blessed to be part of such a wonderful family."

"It really was nice of them, wasn't it? I guess they knew we would love the spiritual feeling this place is surrounded with, as well as having such breathtaking scenery," responded Paul. "But, you know, Katherine, I am the one who is blessed," said Paul, pulling her close in his arms.

He kissed his bride, then, said, "The Lord has given me my hearts' desire. You, my beautiful bride, are what is breathtaking. And to think, you are mine until death do us part."

The next day, they went to the glass chapel to watch the sunrise. Then, they went hiking behind the chapel on winding trails that took them to one beautiful view after another. They arrived back at the hotel that evening, exhausted, but exhilarated.

"I hope Mom and Dad will like our news when we get

back. I am not sure how they are going to take it, but I hope they will be happy for us," said Paul.

"If I know them, they will be ecstatic," said Katherine.

"I sure hope so," said Paul. "But, you know how parents can be about these things. Especially mothers."

CHAPTER TWENTY THREE

Paul and Katherine went straight to Pastor Joe and Eva's house when they came back from their honeymoon. Their apartment was ready, but they wanted to share their news before they went there. They hoped Pastor Joe and Eva would be happy for them.

"Well, hello there, newlyweds," said Pastor Joe, opening the door wide to allow Eva room to greet Paul and Katherine.

"Welcome back," said Eva, going to hug Paul and then Katherine.

"We thought you would be by tomorrow, that you would go straight on to your apartment tonight. But, it's good to see you, of course," said Eva, laughing.

"Well, we had some things to talk with you two about and wanted to do it tonight," said Paul. "Could we all go sit in the living room?"

"Sure, sure. Let me move these newspapers out of the way," said Pastor Joe.

He began picking up newspapers from the sofa, where he had been reading when they drove up.

"Okay, son, here, sit down," he said.

Pastor Joe was wondering what Paul and Katherine had

come to talk about. It seemed a bit unusual to him, to be having a meeting with them so soon after the wedding. He and Eva both sat down and waited for their son to speak. He could see that Eva was having the same thoughts as he was, wondering what was going on.

"First of all, I want to thank you both for the trip. It was as wonderful as you said it would be up there in the mountains. The views were fabulous. I know you have seen it in all seasons now. We could see all the apple trees and dogwoods blooming below in the valley. It was lovely. Thanks again, Mom and Dad," said Paul.

"Yes, thank you, so much, Pastor Joe and Mrs. DuPriest," echoed Katherine.

"It's time you called me Eva, dear," said Eva to her new daughter-in-law, with a smile, patting her hand.

"You're welcome, both of you. We were pleased that you wanted to go there. It's really a special place to the family now," said Pastor Joe. "You know that we took Joey with us one year. He thought it was wonderful, just like you did. He spent most of his time on the hiking trails. Somehow, the rose gardens didn't hold much interest for him," he laughed.

He waited again for Paul to speak, wondering what this was about.

"Katherine and I have some news. We wanted to wait until after the wedding to talk with you about it. We weren't sure how you would take it, so we didn't want to take a chance on spoiling anything for anyone," said Paul.

Neither Pastor Joe nor Eva had a clue what he was about to tell them. They just sat there, waiting for Paul to tell them the news.

"This is something we have prayed about for quite some time. We feel it is something we should do."

"Katherine and I have been offered positions as youth ministers of a church in San Diego, California. We would be able to work together, since the church is so large. There is a great need for youth ministry in a city that size. They would provide a house one block from the church, so we could walk if we wanted to. That would save money, plus give us some exercise," Paul said.

"We wouldn't need to buy another car, because we would be working together," said Katherine.

"The salaries are pretty good, too, because of it being such a large church. We really have prayed about it, Dad, and we both feel this is what the Lord would have us do," said Paul.

"Then, Paul, if you prayed about it and have received confirmation from the Lord, you have my blessings," said Pastor Joe.

"How about you, Mom?" asked Paul. "I know we would be really far away and I have always lived at home until now."

"Well, I am not going to say it will be easy for me, at first, knowing I can't see you every day, but I am happy for the two of you. What a wonderful way to start a new marriage, with a new career. And to think, God has orchestrated it, so you can do it as a team," said Eva. "He put you two together. It was no coincidence you were in the same youth group, or that you shared the same calling. This is no coincidence, either; that they need two full time youth ministers. God ordained this union from the very first date, I believe."

"Well, naturally, we feel the same way. We have talked about that quite a lot. Especially, in the past few days. I was sure you would support us in this," said Paul. "I think the one it will be the toughest on is Katherine's mother. You know, with her dad being gone and all."

"Well, why can't she move out there with you, if she wants to?" asked Eva.

"You know, Mrs. DuPriest, I mean, Eva, I hadn't thought of it, but actually she *could* move out with us, if she wanted to. She doesn't have to work, because Daddy made sure of that, with his life insurance and investments, years ago. She could rent her house here and move to San Diego with us. I am glad you mentioned that. It will make it easier to tell her now," said Katherine, showing signs of relief.

Now that they had received Paul's parents' blessings on their new career move, they went to talk with Katherine's mother.

When they first mentioned the move, Mrs. West immediately became upset and tears came into her eyes.

"Oh, no, Katherine, don't tell me I am going to lose you, too," she said, through her tears.

"Mama, Paul's mother had a great idea. She thought that you might want to move out to San Diego with us. You could, you know. There is nothing holding you here now. You could rent the house, so you would have an additional income from that. And, with the money Daddy left you, you can move out there and enjoy life. And Paul and I would be there. Please think about it," said Katherine, with a note of excitement in her voice.

Mrs. West looked at her daughter, thoughtfully.

"I have never thought of leaving here, but, I'll pray about it, Katherine. Let me sleep on it. When are you two planning on moving?" she asked.

"Well, we told the committee we would let them know by Tuesday. Then, I guess we will just go. We don't have anything to move except our clothes and our personal things. That is the reason we rented a furnished apartment. We rent month to month, so we can be gone within the next three weeks," answered Paul.

By the end of the month, all goodbyes had been said to Paul and Katherine. They had well wishes from their friends at the church, going away parties, and a farewell dinner at Paul's parents' house.

Joey had taken it a little hard, knowing his big brother would be so far away. But, he was in college himself now,

The Power House

and he didn't have any idea where his own future might take him. After he thought about it, he was happy for Paul for his new career.

Mrs. West had found a renter right away. A moving van was to bring her furniture to San Diego. There was a small cottage by the ocean waiting for her at her new destination. She was going to follow Paul and Katherine to San Diego in her own car. Now that the decision had been made, she was actually excited about the idea of a new start in life. Paul and Katherine were equally excited about their new adventure. They knew they were doing God's will. And, Katherine was happy that her mother would be near them.

They waved goodbye early that morning, having spent the night with Pastor Joe and Eva. They were sad to be leaving their hometown, but looked forward to the challenge that lay ahead.

Katherine noticed Paul wipe a tear from the corner of his eye as they drove past the Power House and took the highway leaving town.

Bless him, Lord. Give us your grace to do your will, Katherine prayed.

CHAPTER TWENTY FOUR

Joey was going to seminary. He hadn't planned it that way. He had been studying business education, planning on working at the main branch of the local bank.

He had been in college for three years now. He made good grades in economics, mathematics and his business courses. He had been looking forward to working at the bank. That had been his goal for years.

This particular day, he found his concentration waning, while the professor talked about the subject of the day.

Sitting in biology class, Joey DuPriest felt a stirring in his spirit. He felt as though he was being physically prodded to leave. He bowed his head and listened for the Lord, to confirm in his heart what he thought he was hearing.

As quietly as possible, he got up and eased out of his seat, quietly closing the classroom door behind him. He walked across the campus to the chapel. He noticed when he entered that he was the only one there. The chapel was left open from six a.m. until ten p.m. for the students, and each time Joey had been to the chapel, there were always students there. He knew if he went to the chapel at the Power House he would run into people who would want to stop and chat with him, so he was glad he had come there.

The Power House

He needed to be alone with the Lord right now. Or, maybe it was that the Lord wanted to talk to him. Joey urgently felt the need to pray.

"Here I am, Lord," he said, as he knelt in the chapel.

Then he got quiet, waiting for what the Lord had to tell him.

Joey had been in church all his life, from the first Sunday after his birth. He had often heard his father say, "Wait, and listen for the Lord to speak to your heart."

Joey had always loved the Lord and did his best to walk with Him on a daily basis. As he knelt, eyes closed, he waited, and the Lord began to speak to his spirit. All at once, with his eyes still closed, Joey began to have a vision. He saw Jesus walking along the seashore, beckoning to two fishermen.

Jesus called to the men and said, *"Come, follow me and I will make you fishers of men."*

Joey knew the story well, having read it many times in the New Testament. But, moreover, having heard his father preach on the disciples of Christ. Joey heard the call in his own heart at that moment. In his vision, he saw the figure of Jesus Christ turn and look at him.

He saw Jesus hold out his arms to him, and heard him say, "I choose you, Joey. Follow me, and I will make you a fisher of men." Then, the figure slowly disappeared.

Joey recognized the call when it came. He opened his eyes. There would be no hesitation in his response.

He stood up and said aloud, "I hear your call, Lord. Yes, I will follow you. I want to do your will." Then, he fell back to his knees.

He stayed in the chapel and prayed for over an hour. Then, he got up and went to find the one person who would best understand what had just happened to him, his father.

Joey went to the Power House, where he found Pastor Joe going over notes for his Sunday sermon.

"Dad, can I talk to you for a minute?" he asked, entering his father's study.

Pastor Joe looked up, surprised to see Joey. He knew Joey was supposed to be in class.

"Sure, son, come in."

Joey came into the office, and took a seat next to his father's desk. Pastor Joe got up, and came around the desk, seeing the serious look on Joey's face.

"Are you okay, Joey?" asked Pastor Joe.

Joey's face seemed flushed, and Pastor Joe worried that he might be ill.

"Dad, the Lord just called me out of a biology class. I felt Him tugging at my spirit, so I got up and left class. I went to the campus chapel and I prayed," said Joey.

Pastor Joe stood still, gazing down at his youngest son, waiting for him to continue.

"The Lord called me to the ministry, Dad. Just now, over in that chapel. As I was listening for Him, as you always say to do, I saw a vision of Jesus. He called me to follow Him and become a fisher of men," said Joey.

Joey shook his head slowly, with an incredulous look on his face. He looked up at his father.

"And, I told Him that I am willing to do His will. Dad, I am going to be a preacher," he concluded.

Pastor Joe cried out with joy over what Joey had just said. He reached out and pulled Joey to him, wrapping his arms around him and hugging him, slapping him on the back, celebrating the moment.

"Joey, that is wonderful. Praise God, praise God!" exclaimed Pastor Joe. Then, he pushed Joey back, so he could look into his eyes.

"Joey, your mother told me ten years ago she believed you would be the one God called to preach. But, then when Paul was called to youth ministry, she thought she had missed it, that she hadn't heard from God, after all. So, she

The Power House

didn't miss it, did she, son? You *are* the one the Lord has called. Joey, this is a wonderful day! We need to go tell your mother the good news!" exclaimed Pastor Joe.

They left the Power House to go home to tell Eva. She was overjoyed. She did what most mothers would have done. She broke down and cried off and on for an hour, over the glory God was being given in winning souls through the DuPriest family.

A few years later, Joey graduated from seminary. He was to receive his ordination at the Power House. His father presided over the ceremony.

Katherine, Paul, and their newborn baby boy, Everett, flew from San Diego for the ceremony.

Paul was very proud of his younger brother, Joey. He was so happy the Lord had called him to preach the word.

Joey had been offered an associate pastor position at the Power House. He felt honored. He was also excited to be working for the Lord in the church his father had started.

As Paul was congratulating him on his ordination, a thought occurred to him. He began to laugh.

"What are you laughing about, big brother?" asked Joey.

"I guess from now on, we will have to call you *Pastor Joe, Jr.*," said Paul.

"Somebody already tried that, Paul. It's not going to work," laughed Joey. "No, it's still Joey, or maybe Pastor Joey. Someday, if I am ever called anything else, when I am older, I might want to be called Pastor Joe. But, you and I both know, that, right now, there is only one Pastor Joe. He's standing right up there," Joey said, nodding toward his father. "And, I am very proud to be his son and his new associate pastor. He's one in a million, Paul."

"You are so right about that, Joey. I think we both now realize how blessed we are to have the parents we have," replied Paul.

Paul reached inside his coat pocket. He handed a small

The Power House

package to his brother.

"Katherine and I are proud of you, Joey. We got you this for your ordination," said Paul. "I hope you like it."

"Wow, you didn't have to do that. But it's awfully nice of you, Paul. I'm sure I will like it, whatever it is," said Joey.

He opened the package, and there, nestled in white tissue paper, was a tiny replica of the Power House, made of pewter. It had been made into a tie clip. It had taken some intricate workmanship to make such a work of art, and Joey loved it.

"Thanks, Paul! This is one of the nicest presents anyone ever gave me. You are the greatest. And, the luckiest, too," he said, slapping his brother on the back. "Look at your beautiful wife over there, and that new baby boy. Aren't we all so blessed?" said Joey, putting the tie clip on his tie.

"We are blessed beyond measure, little brother," said Paul. "Speaking of little brother, do you remember how we used to run all over that auditorium during the week, when there were no church services? We used to get our clothes filthy from climbing around under the stage," he laughed. "Then, Mr. Cortinez was given that dream by the Lord, and the Power House was built."

"Yeah, it's amazing when I look around us, Paul. This truly is a Power House, isn't it? Like Dad says, a house filled with the Holy Spirit. Just think of all that has happened here to change people's lives and turn them to the Lord. I want to be part of that now," said Joey. "I want to be able to win souls to Christ. You and Dad are blessed to have been doing it for years. Now *I* have the opportunity," said Joey. "You know, I met a man just last week that needs the Lord in his life. He agreed to meet with me for coffee tomorrow morning, and I look forward to telling him about Jesus, and how He can change his life. I have asked God to help me say the words to change his heart."

Joey put his hand on Paul's shoulder.

"Paul, today begins another era in the Power House. Please pray with me that I can be half the man for the Lord that our father has always been," continued Joey.

"I will pray that for you, my brother, and for myself, as well," said Paul.

Standing in the sanctuary of the Power House, the two brothers took turns praying. They seconded the other's prayer with the word *Amen,* which means *"may it be so."*

Pastor Joe joined his two sons, just as they finished praying. He put an arm on each of their shoulders.

"This is one of the happiest days of my life," said Pastor Joe. "To have you and Katherine here, Paul, along with my new grandson. And, Joey, to be a part of your ordination. It *does* make me feel rather *old,* though, to know you are old enough to be a minister, and Paul old enough to be a minister *and* a father," he laughed.

Then, Pastor Joe grew more serious.

"I told your mother something once, and it comes back to mind today. The Lord gave me the name of The Power House that night after I met Emmanuel. But, you know something, fellas? We had a Power House all along. Back in the community room, we still had a Power House. *Every church that is filled with the presence of the Holy Spirit is truly a Power House.* It doesn't have anything to do with the size of this building. The Lord used our ministry to win souls to Him, even when we were only a congregation of twenty-five members. And, I pray He will continue to use us, as long as it is His will."

"You are right, Dad," said Joey. "I had never thought of it that way, but, you are right about our church always having been a Power House. Dad, this is one of the happiest days of my life, too."

"Joey was just talking about how we used to climb around under the stage at the old church, Dad. Remember how dirty we got, and Mom always called us her *angels with*

The Power House

dirty faces?" said Paul.

"I remember that time very well. The Lord certainly answered our prayers for a larger building. God is good," said Pastor Joe.

Turning to Joey he said, "Say, Joey, do you realize how fortunate you are to be having your ordination in this new building? *If we were still meeting in the school, there wouldn't have been enough seats for everybody!*" he laughed.

Printed in the United States
23737LVS00003B/58-1008